FOUNDATIONS OF FORENSIC MENTAL HEALTH ASSESSMENT

BEST PRACTICES IN FORENSIC MENTAL HEALTH ASSESSMENT

Series Editors

Thomas Grisso, Alan M. Goldstein, and Kirk Heilbrun

Series Advisory Board

Paul Appelbaum, Richard Bonnie, and John Monahan

Titles in the Series

Foundations of Forensic Mental Health Assessment, *Kirk Heilbrun, Thomas Grisso, and Alan M. Goldstein*

Criminal Titles

Evaluation of Competence to Stand Trial, *Patricia A. Zapf and Ronald Roesch*

Evaluation of Criminal Responsibility, *Ira K. Packer*

Evaluation of Capacity to Confess, *Alan M. Goldstein and Naomi Goldstein*

Evaluation of Sexually Violent Predators, *Philip H. Witt and Mary Alice Conroy*

Evaluation for Risk of Violence in Adults, *Kirk Heilbrun*

Jury Selection, *Margaret Bull Kovera and Brian L. Cutler*

Evaluation for Capital Sentencing, *Mark D. Cunningham*

Eyewitness Identification, *Brian L. Cutler and Margaret Bull Kovera*

Civil Titles

Evaluation of Capacity to Consent to Treatment, *Scott Y.H. Kim*

Evaluation for Substituted Judgment, *Eric Y. Drogin and Curtis L. Barrett*

Evaluation for Civil Commitment, *Debra Pinals and Douglas Mossman*

Evaluation for Harassment and Discrimination Claims, *William Foote and Jane Goodman-Delahunty*

Evaluation of Workplace Disability, *Lisa D. Piechowski*

Juvenile and Family Titles

Evaluation for Child Custody, *Geri S.W. Fuhrmann*

Evaluation of Juveniles' Competence to Stand Trial, *Ivan Kruh and Thomas Grisso*

Evaluation for Risk of Violence in Juveniles, *Robert Hoge and D.A. Andrews*

Evaluation for Child Protection, *Kathryn Kuehnle, Mary Connell, Karen S. Budd, and Jennifer Clark*

Evaluation for Disposition and Transfer of Juvenile Offenders, *Randall T. Salekin*

FOUNDATIONS OF FORENSIC MENTAL HEALTH ASSESSMENT

KIRK HEILBRUN

THOMAS GRISSO

ALAN M. GOLDSTEIN

2009

OXFORD
UNIVERSITY PRESS

Oxford University Press, Inc., publishes works that further
Oxford University's objective of excellence
in research, scholarship, and education.

Oxford New York
Auckland   Cape Town   Dar es Salaam   Hong Kong   Karachi
Kuala Lumpur   Madrid Melbourne   Mexico City   Nairobi
New Delhi   Shanghai   Taipei   Toronto

With offices in
Argentina   Austria   Brazil   Chile   Czech Republic   France   Greece
Guatemala   Hungary   Italy   Japan Poland   Portugal   Singapore
South Korea   Switzerland   Thailand   Turkey   Ukraine   Vietnam

Copyright © 2009 by Oxford University Press, Inc.

Published by Oxford University Press, Inc.
198 Madison Avenue, New York, New York 10016
www.oup.com

Oxford is a registered trademark of Oxford University Press

Library of Congress Cataloging-in-Publication Data

Heilbrun, Kirk.
Foundations of forensic mental health assessment / Kirk Heilbrun, Thomas
Grisso, Alan M. Goldstein.
p. ; cm. — (Best practices in forensic mental health assessment)
Includes bibliographical references and index.
ISBN 978-0-19-532309-2   1. Forensic psychiatry. 2. Mental illness—
Diagnosis. I. Grisso, Thomas. II. Goldstein, Alan M. III. Title. IV. Series.
[DNLM: 1. Forensic Psychiatry—methods. 2. Forensic Psychiatry—standards.
3. Mental Disorders—diagnosis. W 740 H466f 2008]
RA1151.H38 2008
614'.15—dc22

2008016305

9 8 7 6 5 4 3 2 1

Printed in the United States of America
on acid-free paper

To our children and grandchildren—Anna (KH), Kerry, Marc and Josephine (TG), and Naomi, Josh, Hillary, and Maia, and Marion and Jon (AMG).
May they live wisely and well, and leave the world better than they found it.

Preface

This book could not have been written ten years ago. Nor could this series of which it is a part. Forensic mental health assessment, along with its foundational science, relevant law, applicable ethics, and associated professional standards, has matured to the extent that a "best-practice" series is now feasible.

This book will describe the "foundational" aspects of forensic mental health assessment. Many of these are applicable across most or all of the types of forensic assessment described by the remaining 19 books in this series. Each of these books will be targeted specifically to address a particular topic in criminal, civil, or juvenile/family law and the best practice associated with the forensic evaluation of this topic.

One recommended approach to using this series involves beginning with the present book, which describes foundational considerations, and then moving to the book(s) addressing the particular topic(s) of interest. We hope this series will be useful and relevant for forensic mental health professionals, clinicians who conduct occasional forensic evaluations, and those in training. We also anticipate that it should be helpful to judges, attorneys, policy-makers, forensic administrators, and others interested in best practice in forensic mental health assessment.

The information presented in this book, and in the series, will be updated as needed. We welcome your comments and suggestions.

Kirk Heilbrun
Tom Grisso
Alan M. Goldstein
March 2008

Acknowledgments

This book, and the series of volumes that it introduces, have been a collaboration in every sense of the word. Each of us was offered the opportunity to write this book and edit this series independently and declined. Together we have undertaken both tasks.

We are off to a good start with this book, and have greatly enjoyed the process to date. We are honored to work on a series that attempts to synthesize a field that we love and has been such a meaningful part of our professional and personal lives.

The American Academy of Forensic Psychology has been an important part of this project since its inception. As the educational arm of the American Academy of Forensic Psychology, AAFP has provided forensic specialists who have been gracious enough to serve as "outside editors" for each of the series volumes. Each of these consultants will be thanked specifically in the book to which they contributed. But AAFP merits particular recognition because of its willingness, as an organization, to provide input on a series addressing topics at the heart of forensic expertise.

Our series advisory board consisted of Paul Appelbaum, Richard Bonnie, and John Monahan. Three of the most eminent contributors in the history of this field, they are ideally suited to provide guidance to a series that is intended to capture "best practice" in forensic mental health assessment. Appelbaum and Monahan in particular provided exceedingly valuable feedback on an earlier draft of this book, the first in the series, for which we are most grateful.

We are grateful also to those at Oxford University Press who have worked with us every step of the way. Mariclaire Cloutier, OUP Executive Editor for Psychology, actually conceived the idea for this series and persuaded us it could be done—and needed to be done. Regan Hofmann, Julia TerMaat, Rachel Mayer, and others at Oxford have been timely, creative, enthusiastic, and very competent—everything we could have hoped for in a publishing team. We thank them all.

Kirk Heilbrun has no grandchildren (for the discerning among you, this may explain why he had the time to be first author of this volume). But he would like to thank his wife, Patty Griffin, and their daughter, Anna, for all their love and support in everything he does. Tom Grisso thanks his wife Donna for ignoring most of what he's doing professionally and helping him attend to matters of greater importance. Among those are daughter Kerry and Marc, co-authors of little Josephine and a yet-to-be-named second volume "in press." Alan Goldstein, father of Naomi and Marion, and grandfather of Hillary and Maia, is third author, based at least in part on these grand distractions. To Paula, who equally enjoys the same distractions, as always, his deepest love and appreciation for her support, assistance (being married to an English teacher has its benefits when authoring and editing), and tolerance.

Contents

Introduction | 1

The fields of forensic psychology and forensic psychiatry have grown very substantially during the last 25 years. The term *forensic*, which is derived from the Latin *forensis* ("of the forum," where Roman legal proceedings were held), refers to professional activities related to law and legal decision making. Forensic mental health assessment (FMHA) is currently conducted by mental health professionals on a variety of criminal, civil, and juvenile issues. The research foundation supporting this assessment has become broader and deeper during recent decades. Ethical and professional recognition of undesirable professional conduct is clearer. In the larger context of the current emphasis on "empirically supported" assessment and intervention in psychiatry and psychology, the specialization of FMHA has advanced sufficiently to justify a series devoted to best practice.

Best Practices in Forensic Mental Health Assessment Series

This series will describe "best practice" as empirically supported (when the relevant research is available), legally relevant, and consistent with applicable ethical and professional standards. We will identify the approaches that seem best, while incorporating what is practical and acknowledging that best practice represents a goal to which the forensic clinician should aspire rather than a standard that can always be met. A number of authors will contribute to this series; these authors have been selected for their specific expertise in a particular area.

This series begins with the present volume, which focuses on foundational, broadly applicable considerations in FMHA. Subsequent books in the series will each be devoted to FMHA on the topic of a specific legal question. The series focuses mainly on evaluations conducted by psychologists and psychiatrists, but would also apply to those conducted by clinical social workers, psychiatric nurses, or other mental health professionals. Each of the books in this series will be relatively short and user-friendly. The 19 specific topics (see next section) were selected by considering several criteria: the frequency with which the particular evaluation is conducted, whether the area is within the expertise of mental health professionals and behavioral scientists, and whether there is a scientific and professional literature associated with the topic. The series editors (also the authors of this first book) exercised some discretion in identifying and selecting these topics, but we consider this identified range of volumes as both comprehensive and representative of the current state of FMHA.

We hope the series will be useful for different groups of individuals. Practicing forensic clinicians should find the information presented in specific volumes to be succinct and current in characterizing best practice. Those who are in training to specialize in forensic mental health assessment (whether in formal training or in the process of respecialization) should find the broadly applicable considerations presented in this book with the more specific aspects of other books in the series to be a useful combination. Researchers and scholars interested in FMHA best practice may find researchable ideas, particularly considering topics that have received insufficient research attention to date. Judges and attorneys with questions about FMHA best practice should find these books relevant and concise. Clinical and forensic administrators who run agencies, court clinics, and hospitals in which litigants are assessed may also perceive some of the books in this series as applicable to their work. Finally, students taking courses in psychology, sociology, criminal justice, social work, law, or medicine should find that reading the present book offers an overview of FMHA, while other books provide more detail about specific forms of FMHA and legal consultation.

Specifics of the Series

The entire series will comprise 20 books. The first will focus on foundational aspects of FMHA that have relevance to FMHA best practice in the broadest sense. The remaining 19 volumes will be devoted to more specific topics: competence to stand trial, criminal responsibility, capacities to confess, sexually violent predators, risk of violence in adults, jury selection, capital sentencing, eyewitness identification, capacity to consent to treatment, guardianship and conservatorship, personal injury claims, civil commitment, employee discrimination and harassment, occupational disability, child custody, juvenile competence to stand trial, risk of violence in juveniles, child protection, and juvenile commitment and transfer. Each of these 19 books will be written using a particular template. The authors will address the applicable legal context, forensic mental health concepts, empirical foundations and limits, preparation for the evaluation, data collection, data interpretation, and report writing and testimony. This will create a fairly uniform approach to considering these areas across different topics.

It is probably most useful to read the present book first, followed by the specific series volumes of particular interest. All authors in this series have attempted to be as concise as possible in addressing best practice in their areas. Rather than have each author cover fundamental considerations followed by specifics, however, we have organized the series by covering the broadly applicable aspects of FMHA in the first book. Reading the first book followed by a specific topical book, therefore, should allow the reader to consider both domains.

We also anticipate that the 19 specific books in this series will serve as reference works for courts, attorneys, and forensic clinicians. When there is a question regarding best practice, the particular book in that area should offer relevant material and analysis. A word of caution is in order, however. These volumes focus on best practice, not on what is minimally acceptable legally or ethically. Courts involved in malpractice litigation, or ethics committees or licensure boards considering complaints, should not expect that materials describing best practice should easily or necessarily translate into the minimally acceptable professional conduct that is typically at issue in such proceedings.

Structure of This Volume

The present book is organized into five chapters. Following this introduction chapter, the second chapter begins with questions of definition, then proceeds to a description of the relevant history of forensic mental health assessment. In the third chapter, we discuss the sources of authority that are important in FMHA. This is particularly important because these sources are somewhat different than the domains that are most important in other kinds of psychological and psychiatric assessment; even comparable domains may be applied somewhat differently. The fourth chapter is devoted to a description of broadly applicable principles and maxims that are important across a range of topics in FMHA. We consider both broad principles and specific maxims, contributed by those in both psychology and psychiatry. Concluding this section, we offer an integrated summary of applicable FMHA principles that revises and updates previous materials on this topic. Finally, in the fifth chapter, we discuss this material as it applies to the question of best practice in FMHA, and offer a brief description of each of the series volumes that will follow.

Note on Gender-Neutral Language

Throughout this volume, we have attempted to use gender-neutral language. Rather than using the more cumbersome "he or she" in every instance, however, we have alternated using "he" and "she" in our attempt at gender neutrality.

The Nature and Evolution of Forensic Mental Health Assessment | 2

Forensic mental health assessment (FMHA) is both a concept and a specialized professional field. The concept or "idea" of FMHA has evolved in the context of practice, rather than having been invented and launched. As a professional field, it has a rich scientific and applied history that provided the foundation for its continued growth today. This part offers definitions of FMHA and reviews its history in two ways: the growth of its formal infrastructure, and a sketch of some of the forensic issues that drove the development of the field.

Defining Forensic Mental Health Assessment

There are at least two ways to define forensic mental health assessment (FMHA). One definition identifies FMHA according to its domain of assessments. A second kind of definition is based on a concept of FMHA that distinguishes forensic mental health assessments from general clinical mental health assessments.

Defining FMHA as a Domain of Assessments

Certain types of assessments have provided the functional identity for the specialty field called FMHA. The types of assessments described in the following discussion represent what we believe is a consensus about the FMHA domain, based on review of major, modern texts that identify the broad range of mental health assessments for courts (Appelbaum & Gutheil, 2007; Goldstein, 2003a, 2007; Grisso, 2003; Heilbrun, 2001; Melton, Petrila, Poythress & Slobogin, 2007; Rosner, 2003).

There are several ways to classify the FMHAs that are identified in those sources. Various classification schemes have value depending on one's objectives, but none are ideal for all purposes. We offer two classifications: systems-based and task-based.

A SYSTEMS-BASED CLASSIFICATION

A straightforward scheme is to divide assessments into their relevance for various systems of justice. The criminal justice system employs forensic mental health evaluations of defendants for purposes ranging from various criminal competencies to questions arising in sentencing. The civil system of justice frequently requires evaluations to determine the presence and relevance of mental disabilities for legal questions regarding individuals' care, protection of their rights, and adjudicating claims regarding injuries and illnesses.

This strategy for classifying forensic assessments encounters difficulties, however, when considering assessments related to juvenile and family court proceedings. The juvenile justice system has a civil history, in that its development was intended to remove juveniles from criminal prosecution. In addition, across the past century, the juvenile justice system in many states acquired jurisdiction, not only over juveniles' offenses, but also over many matters pertaining to the welfare of youth, including their abuse and neglect, termination of parental rights, adoption, and non-delinquent behaviors (e.g., "status offenses") that required the state's involvement in providing structure for the nurturance of children. This history would suggest classifying assessments for juvenile courts within the civil category.

To do so, however, would seem to contradict other developments in the evolution of delinquency law in the past 40 years. *In re Gault* (1967), as well as massive reforms in delinquency laws in the 1990s, rendered delinquency adjudications far more criminal than civil with regard to the protection of constitutional rights and the necessity for due process. Delinquency laws also moved closer to criminal proceedings in their outcomes, in light of trends toward more punitive sanctions (requiring full due process associated with criminal cases) in place of rehabilitative objectives (which once justified the *parens patriae* civil proceedings of the early juvenile court; see Grisso, 1997).

One solution offers a systems-based classification of FMHAs that combines the two parts of the juvenile justice system with the criminal and civil justice systems. That classification is shown in Table 2.1. The first category includes assessments that are performed in criminal court and in delinquency cases in juvenile court. The second category includes assessments found in civil cases, especially involving persons with mental illnesses or disabilities, as well as in the child welfare jurisdiction of the juvenile justice system. The third category includes assessments found in all three systems. For example, jury selection and eyewitness identification issues arise in both criminal and civil cases; they are less common, of course, in juvenile court, but a few states

---

Table 2.1 | Systems-Based Classification of FMHAs

CRIMINAL JUSTICE, AND JUVENILE JUSTICE DELINQUENCY SUBSYSTEM

- Capacity to waive Miranda rights (and validity of confessions)
- Competencies
  - Competence to stand trial
  - Competence to plead
  - Competence to waive counsel
  - Competence to testify
  - Competence to be sentenced
  - Competence to be executed
- Jurisdiction (Transfer to/from juvenile court, to/from criminal court)
- Criminal responsibility (mental state at time of the offense)
- Sentencing (in juvenile justice, Disposition)
- Risk of future offending (aggression; sex offending; recidivism)
  - For pretrial secure placement
  - For placement after adjudication
  - For post-corrections release or placement

continued

CIVIL JUSTICE, AND JUVENILE JUSTICE CHILD WELFARE/ DOMESTIC AFFAIRS SUBSYSTEM

- Civil commitment
  - Mental illness and dangerousness
  - Risk of sex offense recidivism after completion of criminal sentence
- Competence to consent to treatment/research
- Guardianship and conservatorship
- Personal injury under workers' compensation and tort laws
- Employment discrimination/harassment
- Testamentary capacity
- Fitness for duty
- Termination of parental rights
- Child custody

CRIMINAL JUSTICE, CIVIL JUSTICE, AND JUVENILE JUSTICE

- Jury selection
- Eyewitness identification
- Abuse and neglect

allow for jury trials in delinquency cases. Abuse and neglect assessments may occur in all three courts for different reasons: in juvenile courts that have jurisdiction for adjudicating matters pertaining to the safety of children, in criminal courts when criminal charges of abuse are adjudicated, and in civil courts when plaintiffs seek damages for their abuse.

This systems-based classification masks some differences between assessments when they are performed with adults and children. Evaluations for sentencing adults in criminal court may be quite different from disposition evaluations of youth in juvenile courts, and "competence to stand trial" evaluations of juveniles have recently been identified as involving certain conceptual differences from "competence to stand trial" evaluations of adults in criminal court (Grisso, 2005). In addition, some assessments are not entirely distinct from others; for example, evaluations for transfer of youth to criminal court often require an evaluation of matters that are typical for "Disposition" evaluations and "Risk of Future Offending" evaluations.

A TASK-BASED CLASSIFICATION

Another way to classify assessments in the FMHA domain involves the nature of the task that an assessment requires. Table 2.2 offers one way to classify assessments according to the tasks they involve.

Table 2.2	Conceptual-Task Classification of FMHAs

MENTAL STATES, MOTIVATIONS, AND BEHAVIORS DURING PAST EVENTS

- Capacity to waive Miranda rights (and validity of confessions)
- Criminal responsibility (mental state at time of the offense)
- Abuse and neglect
- Testamentary capacity (at a past time when a will was executed)
- Eyewitness identification

DEFICITS IN ABILITIES RELEVANT FOR CURRENT FUNCTIONAL CONTEXTS

- Competence to consent to treatment/research
- Guardianship and conservatorship
- Personal injury under workers' compensation and tort laws
- Employment discrimination/harassment
- Fitness for duty
- Competencies in criminal and delinquency proceedings (e.g., competence to stand trial, competence to plead, etc.)
- Testamentary capacity (assessed at the time of making a will)

continued

- Termination of parental rights
- Civil commitment (mental illness and dangerousness)

LIKELIHOOD OF FUTURE BEHAVIORS AND MENTAL STATES

- Sentencing (in juvenile justice, Disposition)
- Risk of future offending (aggression; sex offending; recidivism)
  - For pretrial secure placement
  - For placement after adjudication
  - For post-corrections release or placement
  - Risk of sex offense recidivism after completion of criminal sentence
- Child custody
- Jury selection

The first category includes assessments in which the task requires a discovery of the mental state, motivations, attitudes, and behaviors of individuals at some point in time *in the past* that is relevant for the legal question. This requirement creates a conceptual similarity across otherwise diverse assessments, in that they all will require collection of data regarding the examinee's mental state or abilities at some specific past time, as well as the circumstances or context of events at that time. Examinees' current mental conditions and abilities are relevant, but they are not determinative, because often they do not directly address the legal question of mental states and abilities at a time in the past.

The second category involves assessments that describe an examinee's *current* mental status and abilities associated with a legal question about the person's present capacities to function in some specific context. The third category focuses on estimates of the likelihood of behaviors, mental capacities, and functioning *in the future*.

The objectives of assessments in the second and third categories are not always distinct. For example, while "competence to stand trial" focuses primarily on present functional abilities, the likelihood that those abilities will be sustained across the future duration of the trial enters into the assessment. This is even more the case for custody evaluations, where present parenting abilities are evaluated in order to make inferences about future parenting.

The classification schemes in Tables 2.1 and 2.2 demonstrate that there is more than one way to organize the domain of FMHAs. Many other classification schemes are possible—for example, regarding special expertise involved in performing various evaluations, populations for which they may be performed (including age and relative importance of psychopathology), and the degree to which the legal questions that they address can lead to consequences that are more or less related to the welfare of examinees themselves.

A Conceptual Definition of FMHA

Examining the term *forensic mental health assessment* offers a way to define FMHA as a concept. What is meant by *forensic?* What does the term *mental health* imply regarding the nature of FMHA? And how does the word *assessment* limit the boundaries of FMHA as a concept and professional practice? Engaging in this analysis is more than an etymological exercise, because it reveals ambiguities in current definitions of the field.

"FORENSIC" MENTAL HEALTH ASSESSMENT

Dictionaries define *forensic* as "pertaining to or employed in legal proceedings or argumentation." FMHAs, therefore, are assessments that are used in legal proceedings. Yet there are several ways one could interpret that assertion.

One could claim that the definition of *forensic* allows *any* assessment to be a "forensic" assessment as long as it is used in a legal forum. For example, if a clinical psychologist assesses a patient in the course of ordinary clinical treatment, and if the clinician is subpoenaed at some later time to describe that assessment in a legal proceeding involving the examinee, our dictionary definition could call this a forensic mental health assessment.

In contrast, many authorities on FMHA limit the scope of the concept to assessments that were performed *with the intention* of being used in a legal proceeding. For example, Heilbrun defined an FMHA as "an evaluation that is performed . . . as part of the legal decision-making process, for the purpose of assisting the [legal] decision-maker or one of the litigants in using relevant clinical and scientific data" (2001, p. 3). By this second interpretation, an assessment is "forensic" not because its results *become* evidence in a court, but because the assessment was *undertaken specifically in order to produce* evidence that would be used in court.

There is little to be said in support of the first interpretation, because it has no particular value. Calling any assessment "forensic" simply because it has been used in court does not advance our knowledge about how to do assessments that will maximize their usefulness by courts. Moreover, it creates a "class" of assessments based merely on where they are used, not what they are. For example, imagine that a school's special education office obtained and used a clinician's earlier assessment regarding the nature of a youth's mental disorder. By the logic of the first definition, the clinician's evaluation would be called an "educational assessment" simply because it had been used by educators, even though it offered no information about a youth's educational achievement and addressed none of the primary educational questions that educators needed to answer.

The second conceptual definition limits FMHAs to assessments that are performed with the intention of assisting legal decision makers. This has greater potential to create a meaningful class of assessments, but only if we presume that the intention to use an assessment in a legal process directs the examiner to do something different from a general clinical assessment.

Specifically, a forensic assessment is guided by the specific legal question facing the legal decision maker. For every type of FMHA, there is a body of law controlling the legal decision to be made. The examiner performing the assessment knows the relevant law within the jurisdiction in which the assessment is being performed, as well as the legal question. The examiner then determines the types of data that are relevant for that legal question and develops an assessment procedure that is designed specifically to obtain those data.

Stated another way, the legal issue forms the "referral question" for a forensic assessment. Most referral questions leading to forensic assessments are quite different from the referral questions encountered in general clinical practice. General clinical assessments typically focus on identifying clinical needs, perhaps diagnosing disorder(s), and formulating interventions in the best interests of the patient. In contrast, forensic assessments focus on helping a legal decision maker decide whether an examinee has certain capacities, abilities, or behavioral tendencies that must be understood in order to decide how to resolve the legal question. Assessments for competence to stand trial, for example, may need to identify a defendant's mental disorder, but primarily for the purpose of identifying specific deficits in abilities that the law defines as relevant for participating as a defendant in a trial.

This definition has important implications for professionals who conduct FMHAs (Melton et al., 2007). First, it requires knowledge and experience in translating the law's definitions of relevant human abilities and conditions into concepts that are amenable to psychological and psychiatric investigation. For example, laws that define competence to stand trial refer to "the capacity to assist counsel." An FMHA that is designed to provide information related to that legal concept must first translate it into more specific abilities that FMHAs can observe and measure.

Second, the relation of the FMHA examiner to the examinee is different from that of the clinical examiner assessing a patient. General clinical assessments occur within a doctor–patient relationship directed toward the best interests of the patient. In contrast, the FMHA examiner's primary allegiance is to the legal process and its decision makers, not to the examinee. This distinction leads to many differences between FMHA assessments and general clinical assessments in the ethical obligations of examiners, as will be discussed in Chapter 3.

Third, the distinction between forensic and clinical evaluations has implications for communicating one's assessment results. Clinical assessments typically are performed to inform other clinicians. Forensic assessments, however, must inform non-clinicians who need the information translated for use in a non-clinical context. FMHA results, therefore, must be interpreted and described in very different ways than clinical evaluations, according to a set of legal rules that were not formulated based on medical or psychological models for the description of human behavior.

FORENSIC "MENTAL HEALTH" ASSESSMENT

The term *mental health* distinguishes FMHAs from other forensic assessments. "Mental health" is only one of the subfields of forensic science, each of which engages in various types of assessments to produce evidence for legal decision makers. Assessments are performed for forensic purposes to test hair, skin, and DNA samples, to examine body decomposition in order to estimate time of death, to reconstruct crime events by examining entrance and exit wounds, and many other types of forensic evidence. The term *mental health* is used to distinguish psychiatric and psychological assessments from other types of forensic assessments.

In general usage, the inclusion of the term *mental health* as a modifier does not restrict FMHAs to assessment of the presence or absence of mental disorders. Included in FMHAs are assessments of various mental states, psychological phenomena, and behavioral predispositions that are relevant for legal questions about human behavior but are not symptoms of mental illness. The term *psychological* would come closer to identifying the questions that FMHAs address, but its use would have the disadvantage of appearing to restrict FMHAs to being performed by psychologists, while the assessment of psychological phenomena is the province of psychiatry and social work as well.

FORENSIC MENTAL HEALTH "ASSESSMENT"

The term *assessment* anchors FMHA in scientific and clinical methods of mental health professionals' evaluations of individuals. The forensic nature of FMHAs involves different referral questions than those that direct general clinical assessment, but the two fields have a methodological similarity rooted in the essentials of "assessment." Hallmarks of assessment in psychiatry and psychology have included a reliance on objective observation and the support of theory and empirical research when interpreting data to arrive at useful inferences. Historically, the general field of mental health assessment has evolved to favor systematic procedures designed to (a) obtain specific types of information, (b) use standardized methods that mitigate examiner bias, and (c) engage in interpretive processes guided by past research on the mental states or behaviors at the heart of the examiner's inferences.

FMHAs conform to those values. Indeed, they tend to elevate those values to a higher standard than in general clinical practice, due in part to the gravity of the legal decisions for which FMHAs provide guidance.

In summary, this analysis recommends a definition of FMHA as a domain of assessments of individuals intended to assist legal decision makers in decisions about the application of laws requiring consideration of individuals' mental conditions, abilities, and behaviors.

A History of Forensic Mental Health Assessment

When did FMHA begin? Some would say that it is thousands of years old, dating to the use of medical knowledge in Roman legal forums. Others, however, might begin the history in the late nineteenth century, when psychologists and psychiatrists began to develop systematic applications of their fields to legal issues. One could claim, however, that it was not until the mid–twentieth century that anything arose that was of actual value or relevance for FMHA as we conceptualize it today. Yet another definition would begin the history of FMHA with the appearance of a cumulative body of literature that identified such a field, which would set its beginnings sometime in the 1970s or 1980s.

Our view is to consider the period from the 1960s to the present as a "modern era" in forensic mental health practice. It was in the 1960s that a critical component for defining FMHA began to emerge. This was the notion that general clinical assessment was not enough. Clinicians were beginning to assert that performing evaluations to inform legal decision makers required a logic and process that modified ordinary clinical methods in order to maximize their relevance for legal questions.

The history of FMHA, therefore, is barely "historical." Published histories of older fields and specialties often do not even try to chronicle the most recent 30 years, because recent events are too fresh to allow us to grasp their eventual historical significance. Were this rule applied to FMHA, we would have little history to describe.

We offer the following description of the development of FMHA in three parts. First we provide a brief view of psychiatry's and psychology's application of their disciplines to law and legal issues broadly, up to the mid–twentieth century. Then we focus in some detail on the development of organizations, literature, and resources during the 1960s through the 1980s, introducing the "modern era" of FMHA that provided its current identity. Finally, in the concluding section, we describe the evolution of selected forensic issues that fueled the modern development of the field.

Foundations for FMHA in Psychology and Psychiatry

Interest in applying psychiatry and psychology to legal issues has a long history. It is much longer for psychiatry than for psychology, but that is not because psychiatry is much older. Psychology developed out of philosophy to take its place as a separate scientific field of study in the last half of the nineteenth century. Similarly, until the late nineteenth century, few physicians or neurologists called themselves "psychiatrists."

EARLY HISTORY OF FORENSIC PSYCHIATRY

Yet physicians for many centuries sought to apply medicine to law, and their efforts create a history out of which forensic psychiatry evolved (Appelbaum & Gutheil, 2007; Gutheil, 2005; Rosner, 2003). Accounts often begin with examples in Roman culture of 2000 years ago involving the use of medical knowledge to solve crimes. The first forensic medicine textbook is said to have been published in 1247 (in China), and Isaac Ray's seminal treatise on medical jurisprudence in 1838 is often used to mark the birth of forensic medicine in North America. Histories of medical expert testimony on mental health issues in law often cite the insanity case of Edward Coke in 1603 and the formation of the roots of current insanity laws in the *McNaughten* and *Guiteau* cases of the mid-1800s. Even Freud dabbled in forensic applications of psychiatry (making an effort to detect the lies of witnesses in court). Establishment of a chair of legal medicine at Harvard University in 1932 served to recognize forensic psychiatry academically.

EARLY HISTORY OF FORENSIC PSYCHOLOGY

Histories of psychology's applications to law (Bartol & Bartol, 2004; Brigham & Grisso, 2003) describe those interests as arising in the mid–nineteenth century, almost as soon as psychology was differentiated as a discipline from the more general field of philosophy. While psychiatry developed in the hospital, psychology's early identity was in the academic laboratory. Students of the earliest psychology laboratories in the late 1800s, especially Wilhelm Wundt's, began applying scientific methods to legal questions like the accuracy of eyewitness recall.

One of Wundt's students, Von Schrenk-Notzing, is often acknowledged as the first forensic psychologist. He offered testimony on the effects of pretrial publicity in murder cases. Von Schrenk-Notzing probably would have considered the label "forensic psychologist" somewhat strange. He is more likely to have perceived himself as an experimental psychologist who, from time to time, used psychological knowledge in a manner that was useful to the law. Another of Wundt's students, Munsterberg, wrote a book (*On the Witness Stand*) in 1908 that described wide-ranging applications of psychology to law, including judging the accuracy of witnesses' recall, crime detection, false confessions, and crime prevention. His ideas aroused widespread attention in the United States. But Munsterberg's treatise offered little empirical evidence to support his views (indeed, it included no citations). This, as well as Munsterberg's arrogance in promoting his profession, actually inhibited the nascent relation between psychology and law for several decades.

An important foundation for current FMHA practices of psychologists was psychology's early emphasis on psychological tests and measures that quantified human abilities, traits, motivations and abnormalities. Controlled observation and quantification were central to the new scientific methods of experimental psychology for developing reliable insights into human behavior. The emphasis was on minimizing dependence on examiners' own judgments, thereby reducing sources of bias and error in describing psychological phenomena. FMHA today includes a special focus on objectivity that encourages the use of structured and standardized assessment methods that reduce subjective error in data collection. Thus the work of the early psychological test developers, such as Cattell, Binet, Simon, Terman, and later Wechsler and Meehl, not only helped establish a science of psychological measurement, but also provided the groundwork for the later development of specialized forensic assessment instruments. Such tools became an important part of FMHA, given its interest in minimizing error in the important task of collecting reliable data to assist in legal decisions of great consequence for individuals in criminal and civil cases.

EARLY HISTORY OF MENTAL HEALTH EXPERT TESTIMONY

The professional practice of providing evidence about human abilities, behaviors, and abnormalities in criminal and civil cases was frequent in the first half of the twentieth century, but in different contexts for psychiatrists and psychologists. The law typically considered psychiatrists the appropriate experts for all matters requiring testimony about mental illness and disability. Psychiatry's foundations were in medicine, which the legal system had relied upon for centuries when testimony about human motivations and capacities was needed. Thus matters of legal competencies, criminal responsibility, and guardianship of persons with disabilities—virtually the whole realm of "mental health testimony"—belonged to psychiatry. Most mental health laws in the United States referred specifically to "physicians" as the professionals solely qualified to testify on such matters. This persisted well into the twentieth century, and remnants of early policies that made forensic evaluations the exclusive province of physicians are still in evidence today in the laws of a few states.

Therefore, while psychologists did testify in the early part of the twentieth century in criminal cases, typically their testimony did not pertain to mental disorders, but to questions about eyewitness reliability or individuals' cognitive abilities. During this era, William Marston, a student of Munsterberg's who specialized in applications of psychology to law, was the first psychologist to receive a faculty appointment as professor of legal psychology (at American University in 1922) (Bartol & Bartol, 2004). His interests were wide-ranging, including studies of jury selection, research that led to the development of the modern polygraph, even producing the popular comic strip "Wonder Woman" under a nom-de-plume. His work frequently brought him into the courtroom as an expert on matters of psychology pertaining to law. One such case was *Frye v. United States* (1923), which produced the legal decision that, in many states, still defines the requirements for the admissibility of evidence through expert testimony.

Child and family law provided another arena in which psychologists were accepted as experts early in the twentieth century. The first juvenile court was established in Chicago in 1899, and almost all large jurisdictions in the United States had a juvenile court within the next 25 years. Most of the new juvenile courts handled not only delinquency cases, but also matters pertaining to the welfare of children (e.g., abuse and neglect and other issues of parental custody). They soon adopted the practice of using psychologists (as well as psychiatrists) to assist in their decision making. For example, some of the earliest "psychological clinics" (e.g., that of Witmer in Philadelphia in the late 1800s) began providing information to their local juvenile courts regarding children's intellectual capacities and social and emotional needs.

Other juvenile courts developed their own evaluation clinics within the juvenile court itself. Chicago's was called the Juvenile Psychopathic Institute, first directed by Healey (a neurologist/psychologist) and Fernald (a psychologist). They provided "studies" of the delinquent child, or what we would now consider comprehensive psychological evaluations (Grisso, 2006; Healey, 1923; Jones, 1999). Their purpose was to assist the juvenile court in deciding the proper placement to meet each child's individual needs for rehabilitation in delinquency and dependency cases. Psychologists predominated in the juvenile court clinics that developed as juvenile courts proliferated across the United States. In addition, developmental psychology's studies of child development and family dynamics contributed to an early acceptance of psychologists as experts in child custody cases.

The law's preference for psychiatric expert testimony in areas of mental health and criminal behavior continued to the middle of the twentieth century. This is not surprising when one considers that *clinical* psychology itself did not develop as a recognized specialty in psychology until the 1930s. Psychologists' involvement in diagnosis and treatment of disorders was encouraged during World War II when the large number of mental casualties of war exceeded the need that could be covered by psychiatrists. The evolution of the community mental health movement of the 1950s provided further avenues for the involvement of psychologists in clinical evaluation and treatment. By the 1960s, many psychologists were working in correctional programs, bringing them closer to everyday practice within the legal system (Brodsky, 1973).

Through all of these avenues, an increasing number of psychologists began to enter the courtroom to testify on issues of mental illness and disability in criminal cases, at least in the states that would allow them.

SUMMARY OF EARLY HISTORY

Taking stock of this brief history, one could argue that the fields of "forensic psychiatry" or "forensic psychology" did not exist prior to the mid–twentieth century. There were some psychiatrists and psychologists before that time whose primary practice involved testimony for courts. But most professionals who sometimes testified in court on mental health issues simply called themselves "psychiatrists" or "clinical psychologists," there being no actual fields or organizations for their specialized practice.

As we will examine in the next discussion, the recognizable features of a field called "forensic psychiatry" or "forensic psychology" did not begin to blossom until the 1970s. This occurred about the same time that the broader fields of "law and psychiatry" and "law and psychology" were beginning to organize. Once organization was attained, the beginnings of a set of concepts and practices of FMHA began to unfold during the 1970s and 1980s. FMHA then acquired much of its more sophisticated science and technology in the 1990s and the current decade. The following brief history examines some of the more important events in the formative period of FMHA development between 1960 and 1990.

Preamble to FMHA: The 1960s

By the 1960s, several professionals were positioned to play an important role in organizing the fields of forensic psychiatry and forensic psychology, which would then begin the process of growth in FMHA methods. Examples of early organizers for forensic psychiatry were Manfred Guttmacher and Jonas Rappeport, who pioneered forensic training in the Baltimore courts, and Bernard Diamond of the University of California, who was working on his creative treatises in the application of psychiatry to criminal cases. The forerunners of organized forensic psychology were not yet quite so identifiable. Many who would eventually play leading roles—for example, Paul Lipsitt and Stanley Brodsky—were just beginning their careers.

INAUGURATION OF MAJOR PROFESSIONAL ORGANIZATIONS

The formal beginning of *organized* forensic psychiatry and forensic psychology can be identified by the inauguration of their major professional organizations. The American Association of Correctional Psychologists was the earliest (1954), and some of its members played a role in the coalescence of psychology and law that was to come. But the organizations that had the greatest effect on the development of a foundation for FMHA were the American Academy of Psychiatry and Law (AAPL) and the American Psychology-Law Society (APLS).

AAPL and APLS began in 1968 and 1969, respectively. That these organizations should arise only a few months apart might suggest that they shared a common motivation. If this is so, the motivation probably involved competition arising from a 1962 U.S. Supreme Court case, *Jenkins v. United States*. An earlier U.S. Supreme Court case (*People v. Hawthorne*, 1940) had established that professionals should be qualified as experts based on their knowledge of the specialized matters relevant to a case, not on the basis of their degree. Similarly, in *Jenkins* the Court ruled that psychologists, despite their lack of a medical degree, could offer opinions as expert witnesses concerning the nature and existence of mental disorders, as long as they could demonstrate that they had training, knowledge, and experience about those matters. Soon after this ruling, clinical psychologists began testifying more frequently in cases raising questions of criminal responsibility and competence to stand trial. A sense of competition was inevitable and may have moved both professions to consider organizing themselves.

It would not be accurate, however, to say that the formation of these organizations was motivated only by their interest in forensic evaluations for the courts. Many psychiatrists who joined were primarily interested in theoretical and conceptual scholarship, not expert testimony. And many psychologists were interested in the development of APLS as a base for scientific study of applications of psychology to law that had nothing to do with evaluations of defendants or litigants. The current history, however, focuses only on the aspects of the fields' development that pertained to the future of forensic mental health assessment.

Little has been written about the early history of AAPL. More is known about the first years of APLS (Grisso, 1991), and it is instructive to describe them because of conflicts that arose almost immediately regarding the nature of what we now call FMHA.

EARLY HISTORY OF APLS

The 13 founders of APLS at the 1969 American Psychological Association convention acquired more than 100 charter members within a few months. Although many members were academics interested in psychological research on legal issues, newsletters in that first year indicate that the primary objective was to improve clinicians' psychological evaluations and testimony. Jay Ziskin, the founder and first president of APLS, had degrees in both psychology and law. He received strong support from the group for his vision of a more empirical approach to forensic assessments, which psychology was uniquely qualified to develop because of its tradition of measurement of psychological phenomena. He proposed that psychology embark on programs of research to develop knowledge that would allow forensic psychologists to base their opinions on methods and inferences that had sound empirical validation.

It was not until Ziskin published the first edition (1970) of his book *Coping with Psychiatric and Psychological Testimony* that his colleagues discovered—in the first sentence of the book—what this really meant to him: "psychiatric and psychological evidence . . . frequently does not meet reasonable criteria of admissibility and should not be admitted in a court of law" (Ziskin, 1970, p. 1). He believed that psychologists as well as psychiatrists currently had relatively little to offer courts, given that their testimony was based largely on methods, observations, and theoretical inferences of no demonstrable validity. Moreover, he claimed that forensic mental health testimony should not be allowed until it had scientific support. Thus his book was designed to provide lawyers with all manner of arguments and questions for cross-examination that would challenge expert testimony on forensic mental health issues. While Munsterberg had tried to put psychologists on the witness stand before they had a science sufficient to sustain their promise, Ziskin's strategy seemed designed to keep them *off* the witness stand *until* they could live up to their promise as representatives of a science.

It is not surprising that members of the organization, faced with abandoning their courtroom testimony until that uncertain day when it could be declared "scientific," simply rejected Ziskin and his strategy. However, as we will see, subsequent events suggest that Ziskin's basic beliefs took root. The need for an empirical base for forensic mental health assessment became the watchword as the field began to develop its identity.

Early Development of the Modern Era of FMHA: 1970–1990

The identity of FMHA in its modern form began to unfold during the 1970s and 1980s in both forensic psychiatry and forensic psychology. Although both professions contributed differently, they proceeded in almost parallel fashion to construct the formal supports for the growth of FMHA. This included (a) *scholarly activities* that created a substantial growth in concepts and methods for FMHA, (b) development of systematic *dissemination* of that new knowledge, (c) development of mechanisms for *training* that would lead to forensic specialization, and (d) inaugurating systems for *review and credentialing* of forensic practice.

DEVELOPING A CONCEPTUAL AND METHODOLOGICAL BASE

As the 1970s progressed, many psychologists and psychiatrists began developing a conceptual and research base on which the future of FMHA would be built. The explosion of creative thought during this time is too large to review here, but the contributions were of three kinds.

First, some of the most significant works of this era documented and described the weaknesses in forensic assessments and typical expert witness practices at that time. Mental health professionals' roles and performance in the courtroom sustained serious criticism, in light of limits in their methods and inappropriate use of clinical information as though it were dispositive of the legal question (e.g., Brakel, 1974; Group for the Advancement of Psychiatry, 1974; Morse, 1978; Stone, 1975). Research on clinicians' judgments about individuals' future risk of violence revealed a greater likelihood that clinicians would be wrong than right when concluding that a person was likely to be violent in the future (as reviewed by Monahan, 1981). Others performed research describing marked inadequacies in the practices of judges, attorneys, and clinicians in cases in which questions of competence to stand trial were raised (McGarry et al., 1968; Roesch & Golding, 1980). Discourse on the proper roles of mental health professionals in corrections and the courts identified difficult issues that needed to be addressed before psychology and psychiatry could assist the courts with integrity (Brodsky, 1973; Monahan, 1980).

Works such as these established the need to set aside the days in which expert opinions by mental health professionals were based simply on extrapolations from clinical practice and were accepted by courts on the basis of deference to the expert's profession. They established the need for a new field of practice that was specifically forensic, complete with its own set of principles, concepts, methods, and science-based knowledge.

Second, several works began providing the conceptual building blocks for a systematic approach to FMHA in certain specific areas of forensic assessment. For example, Monahan (1981) identified a set of factors that would have to be studied, measures that would have to be created, and interpretive logic that would be required in order to develop effective assessments of risk of violence. Grisso (1986) offered an analysis of the essential components common to all legal competencies, then used these components as a template to apply to the development of new instruments for assessing competence to stand trial, competence of parents in guardianship cases, and other legal competencies. Roth et al. (1977; also Appelbaum & Roth, 1982; Tepper & Elwork, 1984) produced a conceptual analysis of legal criteria for competence to consent to treatment, thus providing a set of psycholegal concepts that eventually would be used to guide the development of structured methods to assess patients' capacities in this civil area of competency (see Grisso & Appelbaum, 1998a). In what would become a classic in the field, Melton, Petrila, Poythress and Slobogin's *Psychological Evaluations for the Courts* (1987) offered conceptual clarity regarding these matters pertaining to a broad range of forensic assessments.

This is what had been missing from many earlier efforts to apply psychiatry and clinical psychology to legal questions. Courts that needed to interpret laws pertaining to capacities and disabilities required a different type of information about defendants or litigants than the diagnostic information that served clinics in their treatment questions about patients. Legal definitions and demands needed to be translated into special psycholegal concepts that could structure forensic examiners' approaches to FMHA.

Third, an important development in the new field of FMHA during the1970s and 1980s was the first appearance of "forensic assessment instruments" (Grisso, 1986). These were tools that used new psycholegal concepts as the structure for relatively standardized procedures designed to obtain psychological data relevant to a specific legal question. Clinical instruments for assessing diagnostic conditions, personality traits, and cognitive capacities would still be important in forensic assessments. But the new forensic assessment instruments provided an interpretive bridge between general psychological capacities and abilities or predispositions related to specific legal questions.

For example, measures of psychopathology might be important in determining whether defendants had symptoms that could create deficits in their capacities to assist in their defense. But such measures could not guide the clinician in defining specifically whether and how those deficits impaired the individual's legally relevant abilities. A forensic assessment instrument that would actually demonstrate those deficits could go a long way in helping the examiner explain the relationship between a defendant's symptoms and the deficits in performance on legally relevant tasks. As such, many of these early forensic assessment instruments were patterned after psychological tests that assessed functional abilities (what one can and cannot do in specific everyday domains of functioning) rather than personality traits or disorders.

The first major instruments of this type that were developed with a systematic program of research were the *Competency Assessment Instrument* and the *Competency Screening Test,* both products of a National Institute of Mental Health (NIMH) research grant (by psychiatrist Louis McGarry and psychologist

Paul Lipsitt, but cited as Laboratory of Community Psychiatry, 1973). They were followed in the 1980s by other tools designed to assess competency to stand trial (e.g., *Georgia Court Competency Test:* Wildman et al., 1979; *Interdisciplinary Fitness Interview:* Golding & Roesch, 1983), as well as tools that could guide assessments for criminal responsibility (*Rogers Criminal Responsibility Assessment Scales:* Rogers, 1984), capacity to waive *Miranda* rights (Grisso, 1981), and competence to consent to treatment (e.g., Roth et al., 1982).

Many of the tools of the 1980s have been abandoned or superseded by revised versions. But the growth of forensic assessment instruments since then has been exponential. Grisso (2003) recently reviewed 38 forensic assessment instruments focused on legal competencies alone, and an examination of psychological test catalogues reveals far more instruments designed for assessment in one or more of the other forensic assessment areas in Table 2.1. The early instruments, therefore, paved the way for the development of tools that standardize data collection in a manner that improves forensic clinicians' ability to address legal definitions of human capacities and behaviors.

DISSEMINATING NEW KNOWLEDGE

At the opening of this period (1970), there were no general textbooks in forensic psychology or psychiatry or forensic assessment, and no journals devoted to psychiatry and law, psychology and law, or forensic mental health practice. The foundations for systematic dissemination of knowledge in forensic mental health assessment arrived in the 1970s in the form of book series, textbooks, and specialty journals.

The most significant book series to arise was *Perspectives in Law and Psychology* (PLP). The first volume (*The Criminal Justice System*) was edited by the series' founder, Bruce Sales, in 1977. The PLP series continues to this day, having produced on average a book a year. In psychiatry, an organization established in 1946 called the Group for the Advancement of Psychiatry began (in the 1970s) to provide occasional books in its series that were devoted to issues in law and psychiatry.

Before the 1990s, however, these book series played only an indirect role in advancing forensic mental health assessment. For example, only one of the eight books published in the PLP series before 1990 pertained to forensic assessments. The rest offered legal analytic scholarship, analysis of legal systems, and reports of law and psychology research. Those publications provided some important empirical information about the settings and populations on which FMHA focused, but they did not offer much that was specific regarding forensic assessment methods.

The first general textbooks in forensic psychiatry and psychology appeared in the 1980s. Many of them have continued as revised editions to the present day (Appelbaum & Gutheil, 1991, 2007; Curran, McGarry & Shah, 1986; Gutheil & Appelbaum, 1982, 2000; Monahan & Walker, 1985, 2006; Rosner, Harmon & Ronnie, 1989—later Rosner, 2003; Saks & Baron, 1980; Shapiro, 1984—later Shapiro, 1991; Shuman, 1986, 2005; Weiner & Hess, 1987, 2005; Wrightsman, 1987, later Greene, Heilbrun, Fortune, & Nietzel, 2006; and as the period closed, Brodsky, 1991, 1999).

Many of these new textbooks included chapters pertaining to forensic mental health assessment. However, two general textbooks appeared in the 1980s that were devoted solely to forensic mental health assessments and continued in revised versions until the present: Grisso's *Evaluating Competencies—Forensic Assessments and Instruments* (1986, now 2003), and Melton et al.'s *Psychological Evaluations for the Courts* (1987, 1997, now 2007). The first books on specific areas of forensic assessment appeared in the 1980s as well: for example, Roesch and Golding (1980) and Grisso (1988) on competency to stand trial, and Rogers's books on insanity evaluations (1986) and assessment of malingering and deception (1988). The appearance of forensic assessment texts began to provide an identity for FMHA professionals, helping establish the first clear notions of a consensus (and issues that needed to be resolved) regarding the nature of the field.

The appearance of the first journals in law and psychology/psychiatry provided a forum for research on populations and methods of importance for FMHA. The 1970s witnessed the first issues of most of the present mainline journals for the field (see the first list in Table 2.3).

The earliest of these, *Criminal Justice and Behavior* (developed by the American Association of Correctional Psychologists) and the *Bulletin of the American Academy of Psychiatry and Law* (now the *Journal of the American Academy of Psychiatry and Law*), tended to publish research and discussions related to applied forensic issues. In contrast, *Law and Human Behavior* (developed by the American Psychology-Law Society) tended toward reports of experimental and social psychological research on issues in law, legal process, and the legal system. As shown in Table 2.3, the period after 1990 witnessed an exceptional proliferation of journals devoted to forensic psychiatry and psychology, and the majority of them published information valued by forensic mental health examiners.

Finally, special recognition is due a monograph series developed by Saleem Shah, a clinical psychologist, in his role as director of the Center for Studies of Crime and Delinquency at the National Institute of Mental Health (Grisso & Steadman, 1995). Through the Center, Shah promoted mental health law research—much of it directly relevant to FMHA—throughout the 1970s and 1980s. The Center's series of monographs, written by the psychiatrists and psychologists whose research the Center funded, provided one of the most important resources for the dissemination of concepts, methods, and empirical information about clinical forensic issues during these early years of the field.

SPECIALTY TRAINING AND STANDARDS

Professional standards for FMHA began to develop in the 1970s and 1980s in three ways: (a) the appearance of organizations that offered credentialing for forensic psychological and psychiatric practice, (b) the emergence of specialty training opportunities, and (c) the development of ethical guidelines for forensic practice.

Both forensic psychiatry and forensic psychology developed national credentialing systems for forensic practice in 1978. Forensic psychiatry's system was developed by the American Academy of Psychiatry and the Law, and in later years it was adopted by the American Board of Psychiatry and Neurology. Forensic psychology's system grew out of the American Psychology-Law Society, which funded the development of a separate organization, the American Board

Table 2.3 | Journals Pertaining to Law and Psychology/Psychiatry

EARLIEST JOURNALS

Behavioral Sciences and the Law

Bulletin (now *Journal*) *of the American Academy of Psychiatry and the Law*

Criminal Justice and Behavior

International Journal of Law and Psychiatry

Journal of Psychiatry and Law

Law and Human Behavior

Law and Psychology Review

Mental Disability Law Reporter (now Mental and Physical Disability Law Reporter)

SUBSEQUENT JOURNALS

Aggression and Violent Behavior

American Journal of Forensic Psychiatry

American Journal of Forensic Psychology

British Journal of Forensic Practice

Child Abuse and Neglect

Criminal Behavior and Mental Health

Family Court Review

Forensic Reports (no longer published)

International Journal of Forensic Mental Health

International Journal of Forensic Psychology

International Journal of Offender Therapy and Comparative Criminology

Journal of the Canadian Society of Forensic Sciences

Journal of Clinical Forensic Medicine

Journal of Forensic Medicine

continued

Journal of Forensic Psychiatry

Journal of Forensic Psychiatry and Psychology

Journal of Forensic Psychology Practice

Journal of Forensic Sciences

Journal of Interpersonal Violence

Legal and Criminological Psychology

Psychiatry, Psychology and Law

Psychology, Crime and Law

Psychology, Public Policy and Law

of Forensic Psychology (ABFP). This board developed a credentialing program that was later adopted by the American Board of Professional Psychology as one of its specialties within its credentialing process. In addition, ABFP developed a companion organization called the American Academy of Forensic Psychology (AAFP), of which ABFP diplomates are members, with organizational missions focused on promoting training and resources for forensic psychologists.

Both organizations developed processes to review candidates' training and experience, as well as rigorous written and/or oral examinations that applied advanced standards in forensic practice. FMHA was nourished by this process, as the field's new concepts and methods became part of the standards by which advanced practice was judged in the credentialing process. The credentialing organizations of both professions continue today to promote high-quality forensic assessment practice.

The 1970s and 1980s also saw the development of the first specialized training opportunities for forensic psychologists and psychiatrists. By 1980, a significant proportion of psychology graduate programs with American Psychological Association accreditation were offering courses in "psychology and law," many of them focusing on forensic applications, including FMHA (Grisso, Sales & Bayless, 1982). Not until the late 1980s, however, was there a small collection of postdoctoral programs to prepare forensic psychologists for practice (Bersoff et al., 1997; Otto, Heilbrun & Grisso, 1990), which has grown to over 15.

Psychiatry began developing fellow programs for forensic psychiatry specialization much earlier (Rosner, 1983) and currently has over 30 forensic psychiatry fellow programs in the United States.

Both AAPL and AAFP established continuing education programs by the 1980s. Their primary purposes were to update forensic psychiatrists and psychologists on developments in the field and prepare candidates for board certification. AAFP's continuing education workshops (long directed by Alan Goldstein) continue today and have become the primary source of quality continuing education for forensic psychologists nationwide.

By the end of the 1980s, both forensic psychiatry and forensic psychology were developing special ethical guidelines for their professionals who were providing forensic mental health assessment and treatment. AAPL first published its guidelines in 1987 and revised them periodically (American Academy of Psychiatry and the Law, 2005). APLS collaborated with AAFP to develop ethical guidelines for forensic psychologists, which were first published in 1991 (Committee on Ethical Guidelines for Forensic Psychologists, 1991). They were soon joined by a number of other ethical guidelines in both forensic psychiatry and forensic psychology focusing on narrower areas of forensic assessment: for example, the American Psychological Association's guidelines for child custody evaluations (APA, 1994) and child protection evaluations (APA, 1999).

In summary, by 1990 a great deal of the work had been done to set the stage for the maturing of FMHA. Developments since 1990 are too recent to assess from an historical perspective. But readers will be familiar with the astonishing growth of the field in every way, including the continued development of psycholegal concepts, instruments, research to guide interpretations, and organizational structure in the form of credentialing, continuing education, and ethical guidelines.

A History of Selected Forensic Issues in Forensic Mental Health Assessment

Development of FMHA across the past four decades was influenced by the specific forensic issues that its practitioners and scholars were asked to address. Examining those issues allows us to consider the history of the field based on its intellectual accomplishments, not merely its organizations and literature. Not all types of FMHA can be reviewed here. But examining a limited number of areas from an historical perspective will provide a flavor of the important and exciting challenges that stimulated the continued growth of FMHA. We will examine five areas: (a) future risk of violence, (b) legal competencies, (c) custody of children of divorce, (d) due process in delinquency cases, and (e) quality and admissibility of forensic mental health expertise.

Future Risk of Violence

As FMHA began to crystallize as a field in the 1970s, "predicting dangerousness" was one of the earliest practices for which the field was scrutinized. While the term *dangerousness* is used in legal definitions, clinicians today use it less often, having translated the concept into operational terms describing more discrete endangering behaviors. And few would claim to be able to "predict" those behaviors, given that our best empirical evidence suggests that "estimating their probability" better describes what we can reasonably do.

FIRST- AND SECOND-GENERATION STUDIES

Those insights, however, were far in the future when a set of "first-generation" studies of the issue, during the 1970s, suggested that the false-positive rates for clinicians' judgments about future violence were unacceptably high, often above 80% (Ennis & Litwack, 1974; Melton et al., 2007). Responding to these studies, the American Psychiatric Association (1983) took the position that clinicians' predictions of violence were so unreliable that they should be barred from capital sentencing cases. Yet the U.S. Supreme Court in *Barefoot v. Estelle* (1983) refused to exclude such testimony, pointing out that clinicians' predictions were not *always* wrong and that the trial process could protect from potential error in predictions of future violence.

Researchers then embarked upon a "second generation" of violence risk studies. They were guided substantially by Monahan's (1981) influential monograph that used what had been learned in earlier studies to fashion a number of promising directions for future research. One of these directions was to promote actuarial approaches to risk assessment, thus minimizing error associated with clinical judgments guided only by theory and clinical assumption. Thus began the search for "risk factors" that were empirically related to future violence, examining various populations and both inpatient and community contexts. Hundreds of studies contributed to the search, but the most programmatic efforts were those of Lidz, Mulvey, and Gardner (1993), the "Penetanguishene group" (chronicled in detail by Quinsey, Harris, Rice, & Cormier, 1998, 2006), and the MacArthur Foundation Research Network on Mental Health and Law (described thoroughly in Monahan, Steadman, et al., 2001). Added to these were volumes of studies demonstrating the relationship between future violence and psychopathy, which had been conceptualized by Hare (1970, 1985) in a manner that allowed researchers to identify it using measurable characteristics.

ASSESSMENT TOOLS AND KEY ISSUES

As these research programs succeeded in identifying risk factors that were consistently related to aggression, they began to explore the best ways to combine them for maximum power in estimating the likelihood of future violence. Thus arose the new generation of actuarial violence risk assessment tools that have become standard practice for FMHA: for example, the *Violence Risk Assessment Guide* (VRAG: Quinsey et al., 1998, 2006); the *HCR-20* (Webster et al., 1997), the *Classification of Violence Risk* (COVR: Monahan et al., 2005), and the *Psychopathy Checklist—Revised* (PCL-R: Hare, 1991).

The development of these tools was accompanied by vigorous debate and empirical work regarding key issues in the application of violence risk assessment tools in practice. Among these issues, still active today, are (a) disagreements about the values of a purely actuarial approach in contrast to the use of empirically based structured clinical judgment, (b) the implications of static and dynamic risk factors, (c) the relevance of risk factors for risk management, and (d) the best strategies for communicating the degree of violence risk in order to minimize misinterpretation by legal decision makers.

Similar issues are being debated for a specialty area within risk assessment—the identification of sex offenders who may re-offend.

Stimulated especially by sex offender commitment laws following *Kansas v. Hendricks* (1997), new actuarial tools for assessing risk of sex offender recidivism have gained frequent use despite considerable debate regarding the extent to which their value has been demonstrated empirically (see Harris & Rice, 2003, for a review).

Legal Competencies

The civil rights movement of the 1950s and 1960s brought many legal decisions that provided greater protections to persons with mental disabilities. Among them were cases that defined criminal and civil competencies in ways that protected persons with mental disabilities from presumptions of incompetence based simply on the fact of their mental illness or other disabling condition. New definitions of competence and incompetence required attention to what individuals actually could or could not do. This changed the focus of assessments for legal competencies. No longer would evaluations of clinical conditions suffice; they would have to be accompanied by assessment of actual abilities defined in legal standards for competence.

This functional approach to legal competency grew in application across many areas of law, and legal competencies in both criminal and civil contexts began to acquire certain features in common that could guide forensic assessments for legal competencies. As described by Grisso (1986, 2003), these included an emphasis on functional abilities, the need for deficits in those abilities to be attributable to certain causes, the tendency for incompetence to depend on an interaction between people's abilities and the demands of the situations they faced, and the need for a conclusory judgment and a dispositional remedy in cases of legal incompetence.

In criminal law, cases like *Dusky v. United States* (1960) stirred other courts to begin defining types of abilities that were relevant when assessing competence to stand trial. Responding to these developments, McGarry and colleagues published the first major study of courts' decisions in competence to stand trial cases and the characteristics of incompetent criminal defendants (cited as Laboratory for Community Psychiatry, 1973). Central to their perspective was the need for structured tools to assess functional abilities related to legal definitions of trial competence, and they provided two of them: the

Competency Assessment Instrument and the *Competency Screening Test* (see previous reference).

Their logic persuaded others to develop "competence to stand trial" assessment instruments (e.g., the *Georgia Court Competency Test:* Wildman et al., 1978; and Nicholson et al., 1988; also the *Interdisciplinary Fitness Interview:* Golding, Roesch, & Schreiber, 1984). These tools gained general acceptance and use among forensic clinicians, until a second generation of more sophisticated and specialized instruments arrived in recent years (e.g., the *Competence Assessment for Standing Trial for Defendants with Mental Retardation:* Everington & Luckasson, 1992; *MacArthur Competence Assessment Tool—Criminal Adjudication:* Poythress et al., 1999; *Fitness Interview Test—Revised:* Roesch et al., 1998; *Evaluation of Competence to Stand Trial—Revised:* Rogers et al., 2003).

Civil law saw the evolution of the concept of informed consent, as well as cases that gave patients the right to refuse treatment unless incompetent (e.g., *Rogers v. Okin,* 1979). This created the need to define and assess competence to consent to treatment. Psycholegal scholarship of the 1980s (e.g., Appelbaum & Roth, 1982) provided a conceptual structure for thinking about the abilities associated with competence to consent, and assessment tools for this purpose began to appear (e.g., Weithorn & Campbell, 1982). Major research projects of the 1990s then produced several tools designed for assessing patients' competence to consent to treatment (e.g., *Capacity to Consent to Treatment Instrument:* Marson et al., 1995; *MacArthur Competence Assessment Tool for Treatment:* Grisso & Appelbaum, 1998b). Similar development of structured functional assessments for competency abilities has been slower in other areas: for example, competence of older persons for determinations of guardianship and conservatorship, and competence of parents relevant for legal child protective determinations.

Custody of Children in Divorce

Prior to the mid–twentieth century, the custody of children in divorce cases most frequently was awarded to mothers (Melton et al., 2007). By the 1960s, however, modern divorce law had moved away from automatic maternal preference. Ensuing years found greater use of joint custody and a weighing of information to determine what was in the "best interests of the child." The latter approach increased the need for evaluations of parents' actual parenting behaviors and capacities, as well as assessments of the specific needs of the children involved (Otto & Edens, 2003). Other legal or theoretical standards evolved in the 1970s, such as the principle of "least detrimental alternative" as represented by the "psychological parent" (Goldstein, Freud, & Solnit, 1973). Laws themselves became increasingly specific regarding the areas of parental functioning and child development that courts needed to address in making custody decisions.

These new legal concepts and criteria became the framework within which clinicians fashioned their assessments in custody cases. Instruments to assist in obtaining information about parents' capacities began to appear in the 1980s (reviewed by Grisso, 1986; for an update, see Otto & Eden, 2003). In addition, the 1990s witnessed the development of guidelines for practice in child custody evaluations (American Academy of Child and Adolescent Psychiatry, 1997; American Psychological Association, 1994; Association of Family and Conciliation Courts, undated, later 2006).

These guidelines appeared partly in response to a wave of criticism regarding the practices of clinicians performing evaluations in child custody cases (e.g., Grisso, 1986; Melton et al., 1987; Schutz, Dixon, Lindenberger, & Ruther, 1989). Generally they warned that clinicians had little scientific evidence on which to base judgments about the effects of parenting on outcomes for children. Yet clinicians typically offered expert opinions regarding which parent could best meet children's needs. Those concerns have continued and, indeed, strengthened to the point of recommending severe restrictions on assessment practice in this area (e.g., O'Donahue & Bradley, 1999; Tippins & Wittman, 2005).

Due Process in Delinquency Cases

Before *In re Gault* (1967), clinicians' assessments in juvenile court were primarily "clinical." They informed courts of youth's personalities, predispositions, and psychological needs so that the court could make decisions about their rehabilitation. Only after *Gault's* due process requirements was there a need for "forensic" evaluations to identify delinquent youth's capacities or circumstances related to particular legal criteria for their adjudication or sentencing.

The emergence of the "new juvenile court" stimulated a great deal of research and test development focused primarily on classifying delinquent youth (e.g., Jesness & Wedge, 1984; Quay, 1966, 1987; Warren, 1976). These efforts, however, were primarily intended to create more effective treatment recommendations, not to address forensic issues. Among the first forensic questions raised in the post-*Gault* era was the capacity of youth to waive *Miranda* rights, as well as their characteristics associated with legal criteria for transfer (waiver) to criminal court for trial as adults. Empirical and clinical perspectives on such issues did not appear until the 1980s (e.g., Grisso, 1980, 1981; Schetky & Benedek, 1980) and were only occasionally seen in the 1990s. Indeed, the first text entirely on the assessment of a range of specific forensic questions in delinquency cases did not appear until 30 years after *Gault* (Grisso, 1998).

What changed this picture dramatically was a wave of juvenile violence in the early 1990s that caused most states to revise their delinquency laws in a more punitive direction. The greater legal consequences for delinquent youth caused defense advocates to demand greater attention to constitutional protections for defendants. The consequence was an introduction of the concept of competence to stand trial to juvenile court proceedings (Grisso, 1997), as well as increased attention to the importance of evaluating risk of future violence and characteristics related to transfer to criminal court.

In response to these legal events, it seemed that a subfield of forensic evaluation of juveniles arose almost overnight. Juvenile forensic research and clinical symposia at conventions of the American Psychology-Law Society increased from about 5% of the program in the mid-1990s to about 25% ten years later. Practice guides began to appear (Grisso, 1998; Grisso, Vincent, & Seagrave, 2005; Ribner, 2002; Schetky & Benedek, 2002), as well as new FMHA methods to assess juveniles' risk of violence (Borum, Bartel, & Forth, 2003; Borum & Verhaagen, 2006; Hoge & Andrews, 2002), competence to stand trial (Grisso, 2005), and characteristics related to transfer criteria (Salekin, 2004). After 100 years of second-class status within forensic psychiatry and psychology, FMHA for delinquency cases has taken the spotlight as an exciting, new area of forensic practice.

Quality and Admissibility of Forensic Mental Health Expertise

Each subspecialty within FMHA has experienced its debates across the years regarding the quality of forensic evaluations, and each has been somewhat different depending on the legal and forensic issues that it addresses. But all have focused on the main question that Ziskin (1970) raised at the time that modern FMHA was emerging. What is the scientific base for FMHA, and what type of testimony is appropriate or inappropriate given the limits of that scientific base?

Before the modern era, courts that questioned the quality of FMHA information focused primarily on the training and experience of the forensic mental health expert. But as courts scrutinized the growing use of science experts, they began to demand closer attention to the science base for clinicians' testimony. At stake was the accuracy of information to inform important legal decisions. Due process in criminal convictions, deprivation of freedom, public safety, parents' relationships with their children, and relinquishment of rights of persons with disabilities were too important to rest on opinions that were based on observations of unknown reliability and inferences without empirical evidence for their validity.

Throughout the development of FMHA, the standard applied to admissibility of evidence was one that had been set long ago in *Frye v. United States* (1923), requiring that the method used by the expert needed to be "sufficiently established" to have gained "general acceptance" in the expert's field. Founders of the modern era of FMHA themselves were aware that much of what had gained "general acceptance" in the field was not sufficient, because it did not meet the new field's own standard for a scientific base. In *Daubert v. Merrell Dow Pharmaceuticals, Inc.* (1993), the U.S. Supreme Court issued a new standard for admissibility of expert testimony that came closer to the field's objective, emphasizing the need for the expert's methods to have demonstrated reliability and prior scientific review by peers.

There has been less research on the quality of the actual practice of forensic examiners than on the quality of their instruments (e.g., Nicholson & Norwood, 2000; Otto & Edens, 2003). One of the difficulties in performing such research has been uncertainty about what standards to apply. Similarly, professionals who train our next generations of forensic examiners must have a sense of the field's standards regarding forensic assessments in order to guide their instruction. Ethical guidelines cited earlier in this section offer some guidance. But they focus primarily on professional conduct and much less on specific procedures, methods, and interpretive practices. Textbooks on specific types of forensic assessment focus on the latter, but typically they are written by an author with a particular orientation, so that they do not necessarily represent the field's consensus about best practice.

The need for standards to educate and guide forensic clinicians, and to use in evaluating their performance, motivated the development of the series of which this book is the first volume. There are several different kinds of such standards, discussed at greater length in Chapter 5. First, there are standards that describe minimally acceptable practice. Professional behavior that falls below this kind of standard may constitute malpractice, so this level of standard roughly corresponds with the "standard of care" used in tort litigation. Second, there are standards that describe desirable professional conduct, which practitioners should aspire to but will not necessarily achieve in all instances. Such standards are typically developed by a particular discipline and disseminated in the form of ethics codes and specialty guidelines. A profession develops standards of practice; the law considers such standards of practice and the context of a specific case in determining the standard of care.

In this series, we will describe a version of standard of practice that is somewhat higher: a "best-practice" standard. This type of standard goes beyond what the profession has recognized as adequate or appropriate, aiming to identify what is "best"—empirically, theoretically, ethically, and legally—given current available research evidence and assessment methods.

One should recognize that best-practice standards often cannot be satisfied by clinicians in everyday practice. They are "aspirational," prescribing practices that are the best we can achieve, while recognizing that in many cases we will fall short in our efforts.

The remaining chapters describe the building blocks on which best-practice standards for FMHA can be developed. The third chapter of this book describes the legal and ethical foundations for FMHA, and the fourth chapter offers a set of basic principles to guide FMHA practice. Finally, the fifth chapter offers a concept of "best practice" that incorporates law, ethics, and principles, and introduces the remaining 19 volumes in the series.

Relevant Sources of Authority for Developing Best-Practice Standards

Forensic psychology and forensic psychiatry have evolved over the last 100 years to the point that each is now recognized as a specialty. However, because many practitioners are not trained as forensic specialists, there are a number of practitioners whose formal training has not encompassed FMHA methodology and relevant law. It is not surprising that the quality of forensic evaluations has been to shown to vary widely (e.g., Borum & Grisso, 1995; Heilbrun & Collins, 1995; Horvath, Logan, & Walker, 2002; Nicholson & Norwood, 2000; Ryba, Cooper, & Zapf, 2003; Skeem & Golding, 1998; see also Heilbrun, DeMatteo, & Goldstein, under review) and that the methods used by experts in conducting FMHA vary considerably (Heilbrun, 2001; Horvath et al., 2002; Lally, 2003). Although malpractice suits against FMHA experts are rare (Greenberg, Shuman, Feldman, Middleton, & Ewing, 2007; Heilbrun et al., in press), the ethics codes of the American Psychiatric Association and the American Psychological Association nevertheless make it clear that anyone practicing in a specialization must be competent to do so—"experts" practice only within the boundaries of their expertise.

The need for best-practice standards in FMHA is compelling. This is true for a number of reasons. Forensic assessment can have a profound impact on those who are evaluated and their families and friends. Legal decisions can be made more fairly when judges are better informed. Professional standards can promote competent practice. Since best-practice standards represent the collective wisdom of the profession regarding the most desirable methods and decision making—the approaches that are most relevant, accurate, and psychometrically sound whenever possible—it is essential to consider the sources of authority that contribute to the development of a best-practice standard.

There are four domains that are relevant to informing standards of best practice:

- Law
- Knowledge based upon the behavioral and medical sciences
- Professional ethics
- Professional practice (broadly defined to include theory, guidelines, recommendations, and regulation by professional organizations)

It is true, of course, that summarizing these domains does not convey the full range of legal questions, assessment methods, and ethical conflicts in FMHA. For example, Goldstein (2003, 2007) describes 43 different areas of FMHA practice, each with some distinctive features. However, these areas are the important domains to be considered with respect to best practice. We will now examine each of these sources of authority and the contributions of each to FMHA.

Law as a Contributor to Best-Practice Standards

A major factor that sets FMHA practitioners apart from clinical psychologists and psychiatrists working as treatment and assessment professionals is the need to rely on the legal system—statutes, case law, and administrative code—in designing and structuring FMHA. This includes the methodology, content domains, and work products (written reports and possibly oral testimony; see Ewing [2003] for a fuller discussion of the relevance of law to FMHA).

FMHA, whether civil or criminal in nature, is driven by legal statutes and relevant case law. A forensic expert cannot conduct an evaluation without an understanding of the elements of the legal competency he has been asked to address. For example, an expert is asked to evaluate and offer an opinion as to whether a 10-year-old autistic girl, an alleged victim of a rape, can serve as a sworn witness at trial. This assessment cannot be conducted without understanding the relevant legal statutes and case law, which define the requirements of a sworn witness and distinguish between a sworn and an unsworn witness. An evaluation of that child's IQ, personality characteristics, judgment, and neuropsychological status can explain *why* she might be competent to serve as a sworn witness. However, it is by considering the legal definition of a "sworn witness" and determining the "functional legal capacities" (Grisso, 1986, 2003) of such a witness (that is, what is expected of the witness) that the forensic expert can provide the most relevant information to the trier of fact (the judge or jury) to facilitate an informed legal determination on this issue.

Similarly, a forensic clinician may be asked to evaluate a defendant's mental state at the time of a crime as part of a possible insanity defense. If the forensic clinician provides only a diagnosis and description of the defendant's thinking, feelings, and sources of stress around the time of the offense, this would miss an important aspect of the insanity defense: whether this defendant knew or could appreciate what he was doing at the time of the crime or if he was aware of the wrongfulness of his actions. (In some jurisdictions, an additional relevant consideration would be whether the defendant was capable of conforming his conduct to the requirements of the law). It is, therefore, imperative for an expert to possess a reasonable understanding of the appropriate statute and applicable case law that address the legal referral question because the information contained in these sources shapes the evaluation itself and structures the focus of the report and testimony. In addition, the applicable evidentiary law helps shape how evaluations are conducted and what kind of information can be presented in reports and testimony. Knowledge of such legal procedures is likewise very important in conducting FMHA.

The Law: Defining the Focus of FMHA

The law serves to regulate human behavior. Those who are experts in the behavioral sciences may be called upon to offer opinions regarding the influences that may underlie, explain, or mitigate a person's actions that resulted in a legal proceeding. The findings of these assessments (*expert opinions* if the expert is deemed to meet the legal requirements of an expert witness), which will be considered later in this chapter, have as a goal providing the trier of fact with information that goes beyond the scope of knowledge of the trial judge or the average juror.

As discussed earlier, FMHA practitioners cannot begin to conduct an assessment without first having a reasonable understanding of what the law considers relevant in a specific case. Legal terms are not synonymous with psychological concepts, and the FMHA expert must have an understanding of the legal concepts when designing the evaluation. For example, in a case in which the expert is asked to evaluate whether a defendant was able to validly waive her *Miranda* rights, the focus of the assessment and the selection of instruments used to gather data for an opinion must be driven by the legal standard—whether the examinee can make a knowing, intelligent, and voluntary waiver of these rights. The terms "knowing," "intelligent," and "voluntary" are legal concepts. As such, the novice forensic mental health professional should not make the assumption that a term such as "intelligent" refers to a level of intellectual functioning or cognitive ability that can simply be measured by an intelligence test. As Grisso (2003) cautioned, forensic assessments must be relevant to the legal issue. The forensic mental health expert must "operationalize" the legal competency standard, incorporating corresponding mental health and behavioral concepts into the assessment. In this way, the expert is focusing on relevant legal concepts that are particularly important to the legal decision maker. Testimony characterized by *the presence of* diagnoses or symptoms as its major focus (i.e., "the defendant was schizophrenic at the time of the crime") is at best incomplete and at worst irrelevant, as "the law does not presume that any psychiatric diagnostic condition is synonymous with any legal incompetency"(Grisso, 1986a, p. 8). This was true when Grisso wrote it in 1986, and remains largely true today. However, there have been two important U.S. Supreme Court decisions that draw a direct link between (a) diagnostic condition and legal outcome (those with mental retardation are ineligible for the death penalty; see *Atkins v. Virginia*, 2002) and (b) age and legal outcome (defendants under 18 at the time of the offense are ineligible for the death penalty; see *Roper v. Simmons*, 2005), respectively. It is important, therefore, that the forensic mental health expert possess a thorough grasp of the legal underpinnings of FMHA.

The Law: Deciding Who Is an Expert

In order to testify as an expert witness, the law requires that the mental health professional be accepted as such by the trial court judge. Although an attorney may retain a psychologist or psychiatrist as an expert, it is the court that determines whether this person can offer courtroom testimony. The designation of "expert witness" by a judge grants a special status to the mental heath professional. Unlike the "fact witness" or lay witness whose testimony is confined to knowledge usually acquired based upon what that individual has seen or heard directly, expert witnesses are permitted to offer opinions. They can testify to what they believe, interpreting the data and making use of their observations of the examinee in ways that go beyond a description of the facts. Bank and Packer (2007, p. 423) offer the following example to distinguish "fact" from "expert" witness testimony: "Whereas a lay witness can testify to observing someone 'discussing tax law with his beagle,' only the expert witness can offer opinions or conclusions as to whether the individual was mentally ill at the time."

JENKINS V. UNITED STATES

In a landmark case decided in the D.C. Circuit Court of Appeals, *Jenkins v. United States* (1962), the court opined that an individual is not granted the status of expert merely by virtue of having professional degree. Rather, the expert is asked a series of questions in court by the retaining attorney (opposing counsel and the judge may also ask questions). After considering the potential expert witness's credentials, the judge decides whether the legal criteria for serving as an expert witness have been met. Only then can the expert offer opinions for consideration by the trier of fact.

In *Jenkins,* the court recognized that during this process of questioning (called *voir dire,* meaning to speak the truth, a legal procedure used to determine one's appropriateness to serve a legally relevant role such as expert witness or juror), potential expert witnesses must demonstrate the appropriate background, education, skills, training, or knowledge to qualify as experts, a designation that grants them "exceptional latitude in their testimony" (Ewing, 2003). The concepts delineated in *Jenkins* have been incorporated into Rule 702, Federal Rules of Evidence:

> If scientific, technical, or other specialized knowledge will assist the trier of fact to understand the evidence or to determine a fact in issue, a witness qualified as an expert by knowledge, skill, experience, training, or education, may testify thereto in the form of an opinion or otherwise, if (1) the testimony is based upon sufficient facts or data, (2) the testimony is the product of reliable principles and methods, and (3) the witness has applied the principles and methods reliably to the facts of the case. [*See* http://www.law.cornell.edu/ rules/fre/ACRule702.htm.]

CRITERIA FOR EXPERTISE

Because the scope of FMHA encompasses a wide range of legal issues, the concept of a "generic" expert does not exist. A forensic mental health professional cannot possibly be an expert on every legal issue that courts litigate. It must be demonstrated that the proposed expert possesses the *specialized* education, experience, knowledge, training, or skill relevant to the *specific* legal issue to be decided by the court. A best-practice standard recognizes that, before accepting a case, the mental health professional should be confident that she satisfies these criteria for expertise in the context of this case. Forensic mental health experts should possess the specialized knowledge required to participate in the case (e.g., sentencing, mental state at the time of the crime, employment discrimination, child custody) and be familiar with individuals of similar age, characteristics, and legal status to those of the examinee.

The Law: Determining Admissibility of Expert Testimony on a Specific Topic

If recognized by the court as an expert, the forensic mental health professional may be required to indicate the nature of the testimony to be offered and the methodology upon which the opinions are based. This is more likely if the proposed testimony would address a topic not usually considered by the court (e.g., the likelihood that a defendant has given a false confession) or involves the use of a specialized tool by the expert as part of the FMHA (e.g., instruments related to evaluating the likelihood sexual violence recidivism). The law has requirements that must be met in order for testimony to be admissible. The major purpose of such evidentiary criteria is "to prevent unqualified experts from testifying in the courtroom on the basis of irrelevant or inadequate evidence" (Weissman & DeBow, 2003, p. 47). Experts must ensure that, when a case is initially accepted, their approach to FMHA is such that their evaluation and oral testimony would meet the legal standard for admissibility, both in substance and in methodology.

FRYE AND DAUBERT STANDARDS

Testimony offered by forensic mental health experts must rely, at least in part, on science (Ewing, 2003). In *Frye v. United States* (1923), the court held that in order for expert testimony to be admissible, it "must be sufficiently established to have gained general acceptance in the particular field in which it belongs" (p.10). The *Frye* standard was incorporated into federal and state jurisdictions. It served as the most influential standard for admissibility of expert testimony until 1993, when the U.S. Supreme Court decided that the more expansive criteria for the admissibility of expert testimony described in the Federal Rules of Evidence superseded *Frye* in federal jurisdictions (*Daubert v. Merrell Dow Pharmaceuticals,* 1993). The Court held that the *Frye* test was too restrictive. Instead, it should be replaced by a broader standard based on whether such testimony would be likely to assist the trier of fact and if such testimony and the methods upon which it is based were reliable and relevant. As such, in all federal courts and in those states that have adopted the *Daubert* standard, testimony must be both substantively and methodologically consistent with scientific procedures. Unlike *Frye* jurisdictions, in which the court must only determine whether expert testimony is based on techniques that are generally accepted, judges in *Daubert* jurisdictions must play a more active role. The judge may be asked to consider a range of factors under *Daubert*. These include whether the theory or technique in question can be tested, whether it has been tested, whether it has been subjected to peer review and publication, its known or potential error rate, the existence and maintenance of standards controlling its operation, and whether it has attracted widespread acceptance within a relevant scientific community. The consideration is flexible and must focus on principles and methodology rather than conclusions (1993).

Subsequently, the U.S. Supreme Court (in *General Electric Co. v. Joiner*, 1997) held that the trial court judge's decision cannot be overruled by an appeals court (except in rare cases of abuse of judicial discretion). Preliminary hearings addressing the *Frye* or *Daubert* requirements are therefore critical to any criminal or civil trial; if the legal standard is not met, the forensic expert will not be permitted to testify. Whether practicing in a *Frye* or *Daubert* jurisdiction, forensic mental heath experts should be aware of the specific evidentiary law that governs the admissibility of their testimony. As part of a best-practice standard, experts should anticipate that testimony on an unusual or controversial topic or the use of a specialized tool may be subject to legal challenge. A best-practice standard would thus require forensic mental health professionals to be experts in both practice and the underlying science.

The Law: Setting Limits on Expert Testimony

The legal system sets evidentiary criteria used to determine the admissibility of expert testimony. It also sets legal limits on the subject matter of the testimony itself. There are two particularly significant legal limitations on the testimony of forensic mental health experts: reliance on third party information as a source of data in forming opinions, and whether experts can testify to the ultimate issue (the legal question to be decided by the trier of fact).

THIRD PARTY INFORMATION

Forensic assessments differ significantly from traditional clinical evaluations in the presence of substantial external incentives to deceive the forensic examiner. To manage this challenge, experts must consider third party information—reviewing records and interviewing others (collateral informants) familiar with the examinee and the issue in question—to corroborate data provided by the litigant in testing and interviews. Third party information is, from a legal perspective, hearsay. The expert using such information must rely on the indirect sources of records and interviews with collateral observers. While fact witnesses are not permitted to testify about hearsay information, the rules are somewhat different for forensic mental health experts. The

Federal Rules of Evidence allow the use and admissibility of third party information:

> The facts or data in the particular case upon which an expert bases an opinion or inference may be those perceived by or made known to the expert at or before the hearing. If of a type reasonably relied upon by experts in the particular field in forming opinions or inferences upon the subject, the facts or data need not be admissible in evidence in order for the opinion or inference to be admitted. Facts or data that are otherwise inadmissible shall not be disclosed to the jury by the proponent of the opinion or inference unless the court determines that their probative value in assisting the jury to evaluate the expert's opinion substantially outweighs their prejudicial effect. [Rule 703; *see* http://www.law.cornell.edu/rules/fre/ ACRule703.htm.]

There are certain advantages provided by the use of third party information in FMHA. Such information can (a) increase the accuracy of the findings; (b) increase the face validity of the evaluation and testimony; (c) improve communication with attorneys and judges regarding the assessment; and (d) provide information to the forensic mental health expert as to the role of deliberate distortion by the examinee (Heilbrun, Warren, & Picarello, 2003).

Such use of third party information would probably be admissible under *Frye* as a method that is generally accepted. Although the question of the admissibility of third party information could be more complex in *Daubert* jurisdictions, it does not seem to have been raised with any frequency. Heilbrun (1996) noted, in a review of 276 appellate cases involving *Daubert* challenges in the three years following the original decision, that none of these challenges involved the use of third party information. In a review of the legal and ethical issues associated with using third party information in FMHA, Otto, Slobogin, and Greenberg (2007) indicated that "most courts are willing to permit testimony based on virtually any third-party information, even when it is from a source whose credibility may be questionable" (p. 192). They cited a number of decisions in which hearsay statements were deemed acceptable, including statements offered by "a government agent (*United States v. Sims,* 1973, p. 149), a codefendant (*United States v. Wright,* 1986, p. 1100), and reports of nonclinical staff (*United States v. Bramlet,* 1987, p. 856)."

However, a New York State criminal case, *People v. Goldstein* (2005) added a major wrinkle for forensic experts conducting FMHA in that state and may eventually be adopted in other jurisdictions. Relying on a U.S. Supreme Court decision (*Crawford v. Washington,* 2004) in which it was held that the government could not introduce statements of a testimonial nature made by an unavailable witness, the New York court indicated that unless the corroborative informant is available to testify (and be cross-examined), experts cannot testify to such third party statements. Forensic mental health experts should continue to include third party information in their evaluations. But in jurisdictions that adopt *Goldstein,* they must be particularly cautious in their interviews of third parties. Before conducting such interviews, they should be confident that anyone interviewed as a collateral source of information will be available for trial—or the expert must be prepared to explain why that person will not be available to testify at trial.

ULTIMATE ISSUE TESTIMONY
In some jurisdictions, the law also prohibits testimony on the ultimate issue (the legal question to be answered by the trier of fact). There continues to be an ongoing debate about how far an expert can go in stating an opinion that is at the heart of ultimate issues such as whether a defendant was capable of waiving *Miranda* rights, whether the defendant was insane at the time of a crime, or which parent should be awarded custody (Grisso, 1986; Morse, 1999; Poythress, 1982; Rogers & Ewing, 1989; Slobogin, 1989). There have been ethical, empirical, and legal justifications offered in support of barring ultimate issue testimony, but this is not a question that has been settled in the field (Heilbrun, 2001).

According to Rule 704(b) of the Federal Rules of Evidence:

> No expert witness testifying with respect to the mental state or condition of a defendant in a criminal case may state an opinion or inference as to whether the defendant did or did not have the mental state or condition constituting an element of the crime charged or of a defense thereto. Such ultimate issues are matters for the trier of fact alone.

In federal jurisdictions on the issue of sanity at the time of the offense, forensic mental health experts are prohibited from testifying to both the *ultimate* issue (i.e., "The defendant was, in my opinion, insane at the time of the crime") and the *penultimate* opinion, (i.e., "In my opinion, at the time of the crime the defendant suffered from a severe mental disease or defect, and as a result, was unable to appreciate the nature and quality or the wrongfulness of his act" [as defined by the federal Insanity Defense Reform Act, 18, U.S.C. Sec. 17, 1984]). However, in federal court, an expert is permitted to testify as to the defendant's diagnosis, behavior, and mental state at the time of the offense. All federal courts have interpreted this statute to exclude testimony on strict *mens rea* (whether the defendant possessed the requisite mental state at the time of the crime to be held legally culpable) (Goldstein, Morse, & Shapiro, 2003). However, forensic mental health experts are permitted to testify as to a defendant's personality characteristics and signs of mental abnormality as long as these symptoms and behaviors are not connected in the testimony to the legal elements required to establish *mens rea* (*United States v. Cameron,* 1990; *United States v. Childress,* 1995; *United States v. Pohlot,* 1987).

A judge may exclude ultimate opinion testimony even in jurisdictions that allow it. Such a judge might reason that (a) these opinions go beyond the expertise of the forensic clinician, and (b) such testimony represents legal conclusions that the trier of fact has been charged with deciding. (It should be noted that when the trier of fact reaches a verdict, it is referred to as a "fact"; experts are restricted to presenting "opinions"). But in most jurisdictions, forensic experts are allowed to offer ultimate legal opinions (Goldstein, Morse, & Shapiro, 2003).

A best-practice standard would require that forensic mental health experts be familiar with the applicable law on ultimate opinion testimony. Such testimony can usurp the role of the fact-finder by adding moral and community-value-laden elements to the scientific and clinical expertise required of the forensic clinician (Morse, 1999; Melton et al., 2007), answering the question that cannot be answered without interjecting such values: How impaired must an individual be in order to be legally insane? Tillbrook, Mumley, and Grisso (2003) have reasoned that, because there is no scientific or clinical basis to measure or objectify such legal concepts as "sufficient present ability," then "mental health professionals cannot properly draw conclusions about how much incapacity, dangerousness, etc. is enough to meet the legal standard" (p. 83). They argue that ultimate opinions on such issues are inappropriate and illogical, threatening the integrity of the legal process and the credibility of forensic mental health professions. Similarly, Heilbrun (2001) asks, "How much ability is legally enough?" (p. 223). In some states and in federal jurisdictions, however, applicable rules on FMHA (particularly those focusing on trial competency) require experts to offer ultimate opinions on the ultimate legal issue. As well, there may be policy or practice considerations in some hospitals or court clinics in the public sector that require evaluators to express an ultimate issue conclusion in order to trigger a certain response (e.g., a hospital report that did not give an opinion that the defendant was competent to stand trial might not result in the defendant's being transported back to court for disposition of charges). Finally, several psycholegal scholars (e.g., Rogers & Ewing, 1989; Rogers & Shuman, 2000) have argued in favor of providing ultimate legal opinions, reflecting the absence of consensus in the field on this question.

The Law and the Threshold for Offering an Expert Opinion

A forensic mental health professional is accorded special status, permitting him to offer opinions, when recognized as an expert by the court. Although such opinions may fall short of addressing the ultimate issue, opinions regarding the findings of the FMHA relevant to the legal question are admitted into the record to be considered by the trier of fact. In soliciting opinions in court, attorneys frequently ask the expert whether the opinions the expert has reached meet a certain level of confidence. The question typically is asked as follows: "Have you formed an opinion as to [the matter in question] to a reasonable degree of psychological/medical certainty?" The legal and practice implications of the concept "psychological/medical certainty" should be thoroughly considered by the testifying expert before responding to this question.

Experts in the "hard sciences" are typically asked whether opinions they have reached rise to the level of a reasonable degree of *scientific* certainty. However, it may be that scientific certainty is not the appropriate standard to use for FMHA. The subject matter of psychology is based upon scientific research. However, FMHA incorporates both scientific data (using, for instance, results from psychological tests and specialized forensic assessment instruments) and idiographic data (obtained from a single individual, the litigant in the case). Experts should rely on data from peer-reviewed scientific studies whenever possible—but these data must still be applied to the unique facts of the case and the specific features of the litigant. Moreover, there are some aspects of scientific decision making that do not correspond well with the FMHA process. It would not be meaningful, for instance, to use the conventional scientific probability of .05 with respect to individual results.

Forensic mental health experts typically are asked to respond to questions focusing on psychological certainty (or professional certainty, or medical certainty), a concept conventionally accepted in evidentiary law but whose meaning is not precise. A series of law review articles has addressed the imprecision of this standard. Lewin commented, "Although judges expect, and sometimes insist, that expert opinions be expressed with 'reasonable medical certainty,' and although attorneys ritualistically intone the phrase, no one knows what it means! No consensus exists among judges, attorneys, or academic commentators as to whether 'reasonable medical certainty' means 'more probable than not' or 'beyond a reasonable doubt' or something in between" (1998, p. 380). Similarly, Faigman noted that the term *medical/psychological certainty* "has no empirical meaning and is simply a mantra repeated by experts for purposes of legal decision makers who similarly have no idea what it means. Case-specific conclusions, in fact, appear to be based on an admixture of knowledge of the subject, experience over the years, commitment to the client or cause, intuition, and blind faith. Science it is not" (2006, p. 1224). (See also Craig, 1999; Bradford, 2001.)

In *Hahn v. Union Pacific Railroad* (2004), an Illinois state appellate court observed that there is "no magic to the phrase itself. The phrase provides legal perspective to medical testimony and signals to the jury that a medical opinion is not based on mere guess or speculation. It is of no consequence that a medical expert fails to use this phrase if the expert's testimony reveals that his opinions are based upon specialized knowledge and experience and recognized medical thought." In this particular case, Union Pacific Railroad contended that Hahn's attorney had not prefaced questions to his expert with the phrase "based upon a reasonable degree of medical certainty." The appellate court added that when experts are not able to offer "an unequivocal opinion," then opinions based upon knowledge and experience are distinct from those based upon mere speculation.

It seems clear that, "reasonable degree of psychological/medical/ professional certainty" has no precise meaning. But there remains the question of the threshold to be applied in FMHA in reaching opinions. In an informal survey of psychologists who are board certified in forensic psychology by the American Board of Professional Psychology, conducted in July 2007 by one of the authors (A. Goldstein), a range of responses was received regarding both the meaning of "reasonable psychological certainty" and the level of certainty required to proffer an opinion. In general, respondents cautioned against confusing this legal concept with the conventionally accepted level of scientific certainty reflecting the probability of a Type 1 error (.05 level of significance). Estimates proposed by respondents to this survey as to the percentage of confidence required to proffer an opinion ranged from "above 50% certainty" to "above 80%." As such, it appears that reliance on a specific threshold, expressed in terms of a percentage of confidence or certainty, is not meaningful for FMHA experts when deciding whether an opinion can be relied upon. Many forensic psychologists who responded to this informal survey emphasized that opinions should be grounded in the data, not based on speculation, a recognition that expert opinions must be based on information that can be explained and cited in reports and testimony.

BEST-PRACTICE STANDARD

A best-practice standard requires that forensic mental health experts consider the standard associated with proffering an opinion. It is possible that the expert will be asked a question that incorporates this standard as part of their testimony. Even if there is no such question in testimony, or if the FMHA report is entered into evidence without oral testimony, it is still important that the expert be aware of the basis for the opinion and the level of confidence required to form it. We propose the following threshold:

> Opinions should be data based, including thorough consideration given to all sources of information: comprehensive notes of litigant's interview responses; results of all psychological tests and instruments; information provided by third parties; and a review of records. Relevant studies, published in peer review journals on issues related to the specific case, should be considered as well. Findings should be examined for consistency within and between data sources; major inconsistencies may preclude forming an opinion. Whenever possible, opinions should incorporate sources with established reliability, and with validity for purposes consistent with the present evaluation. Alternative opinions conflicting with the opinions reached, should be considered, and rejected when they are less consistent with all of the information available to the expert.

Such a best-practice standard would promote an FMHA methodology that is careful, systematic, and data-driven. This is not to suggest that forensic experts substitute this standard for the legally conventional "reasonable degree of certainty," or even offer to define the reasonable certainty standard if they are not asked to do so. Such attempts may yield benefits that are far outweighed by costs (see, e.g., Morse, 1982; Poythress, 1982). But using such a standard, and providing it to explain one's methodology when asked, is well within the spirit of FMHA best practice.

The Law Affecting the Regulation of FMHA Practice

State and provincial licensing laws regulate the practice of forensic mental health professionals in a number of ways. Each jurisdiction sets its own licensing requirements. Licenses are largely generic; states and provinces license psychologists and physicians but do not otherwise certify specific expertise, leaving such certification to specialty boards recognized by professional associations. Jurisdictions typically limit the practice of mental health professions under applicable licensing regulations and ethics codes to activities that fall within the boundaries of the licensee's background and training.

SPECIALTY CERTIFICATION AND TRAINING

There are, however, a few jurisdictions that offer limited specialty certification. For example, in the Commonwealth of Massachusetts, psychologists employed or contracted by Departments of Mental Health or Corrections to conduct public-sector, court-ordered forensic assessments must become "designated forensic psychologists" or "certified juvenile court clinicians." To earn this designation, the psychologist must undergo a review of prior work and pass a written examination. In Michigan, state employees who conduct court-appointed trial competency assessments can become "certified forensic psychologists." If they also conduct criminal responsibility assessments, they can be designated "consulting forensic examiners." Applicants in Michigan must meet requirements involving supervision, experience, and participation in a mock trial, although a formal written examination is not given. Missouri has established training, experience, and supervision criteria for all psychologists or physicians employed or contracted by the Department of Mental Health to conduct trial competence or criminal responsibility assessments. Those who meet these standards may be required to take a written or oral examination or both and become "certified forensic examiners." In some circumstances, any of Missouri's requirements can be waived if the committee agrees that applicants have acquired equivalent experience or knowledge of forensic assessments.

There are other jurisdictions that offer specialized training but not certification. In Virginia, forensic mental health experts who conduct evaluations of competence to stand trial, sanity at the time of the offense, or sentencing are required to complete training approved by that state's Commissioner of Mental Health, Mental Retardation and Substance Abuse Services and conducted by the Institute of Law, Psychiatry, and Public Policy at the University of Virginia. Specialized forensic training for mental health professionals is provided in Florida by the Florida Mental Health Institute, University of South Florida.

CONDUCTING FMHA OUT OF STATE

The issue of conducting FMHA out of state (in jurisdictions in which the practitioner is not licensed) is a controversial one. If the examinee travels to the state in which the practitioner is licensed for the assessment, this problem may be avoided. However, in criminal cases in which defendants are unable to post bond and remain incarcerated, this is not practical. A number of forensic mental health experts have discussed the issue of conducting FMHA in jurisdictions in which the professional is not licensed (e.g., Drogin, 1999; Shuman, Cunningham, Connell, & Reid, 2003; Tucillo, DeFilippis, Denny, & Dsurney, 2002; Yantz, Bauer, & McCaffrey 2006). Drogin (1999) reported that 32 of 50 states offered ways in which mental health professionals not licensed in that jurisdiction might be deemed eligible to practice on a temporary basis, and suggested how attorneys might be able to obtain temporary permission for their experts to conduct FMHA. Tucillo and colleagues (2002) noted that 40 of 50 states permitted some form of temporary license, most of which carried specific time restrictions. Shuman and colleagues (2003) discussed the potential pitfalls in conducting such evaluations in states in which the professional was unlicensed, and proposed a model to address this problem. Most recently, Yantz et al. (2006) found that all 10 Canadian provinces and territories surveyed allowed temporary licenses, as did 40 of the 50 states in the United States. However, they added that time limits and specific requirements for temporary licenses varied widely, from five days a year in Vermont to up to one year in Massachusetts. It is clear that forensic mental health professionals conducting FMHA should be familiar with licensing requirements in all jurisdictions in which they conduct evaluations.

Behavioral and Medical Sciences Contributing to Best-Practice Standards

The behavioral and medical sciences provide the conceptual and empirical foundations on which FMHA is based. This knowledge base provides data, tests, and specialized tools that allow forensic mental health experts to incorporate measures with established reliability and validity into their forensic assessment. In addition, it provides an empirical basis for interpreting the data offered by experts in their reports and testimony.

Scientific Knowledge Providing the Theoretical Basis for FMHA

As discussed by Goldstein (2003), college students taking their first psychology course quickly learn that behavior falls on a continuum, often represented by the normal distribution curve. Distribution curves serve as statistical and graphical representations of one fundamental underpinning of the discipline of psychology. Most behavior cannot accurately be classified as falling into one of two discrete categories. Rather, behavior is complex and multi-determined. Students who complete advanced degrees, whether in psychology or medicine, come to accept the concept of behavior as complex and widely distributed. However, in forensic mental health practice, these same professionals work within a legal system that uses a decision-making system in which the options are typically dichotomous and forced-choice. The law usually requires the trier of fact to reach verdicts that fall within one of two discrete categories (e.g., "sane" versus "insane," "competent to stand trial" versus "incompetent to stand trial," "liable" versus "not liable"). The theoretical and scientific aspects of psychology and psychiatry should suggest to forensic mental health professionals that they would be wise to avoid using only dichotomies, however consistent such dichotomous classifications might be with the structure of legal decision making. FMHA opinions should reflect the complexity of the findings, contradictions, and variations contained in the data, and avoid summarizing and categorizing the results of the evaluation in reductionistic fashion.

THEORETICAL MODELS FOR CONDUCTING FMHA

Texts published in the 1980s and 1990s provide a relatively consistent theoretical model for conducting FMHA. In general, authors recommended that FMHA be driven by the appropriate legal statutes and case law that underlie the referral question. They emphasized that objective measures (including traditional tests and forensic assessment instruments) should be used in conducting evaluations whenever possible. Authors also recommended that multiple sources of information be used (Blau, 1984; Grisso, 1986; Gutheil & Appelbaum, 1982; Melton, Petrila, Poythress, & Slobogin, 1987, 1997; Shapiro, 1984, 1991). More recently, these recommendations have been reinforced and elaborated (Goldstein, 2003a, 2007; Grisso, 2003; Heilbrun, 2001; Heilbrun, Marczyk, & DeMatteo, 2002; Heilbrun, Warren, & Picarello, 2003; Melton, Petrila, Poythress, & Slobogin, 2007; Otto, Slobogin, & Greenberg, 2007).

For over 20 years, Grisso's text, *Evaluating Competencies* (1986a, 2003) has provided the principal theoretical model that structures and guides FMHA. Grisso (1986a) argued that most of the discontent with FMHA fell within three domains:

1. *ignorance* of the laws that drive the evaluation, and the resulting irrelevance of the report and opinion;

2. *intrusion* into matters of the law, including opinions that address the ultimate legal question; and

3. *insufficiency* (reliance on inadequate information upon which to base opinions) and *incredibility* (speculation rather than data-based findings).

The model for conducting FMHA originally proposed by Grisso (1986a) emphasizes the need to appropriately identify and understand the "legal competency" construct (the legal statute and case law relevant to the legal referral question) and to "operationalize" this construct so that its legal components are expressed in terms of "functional abilities," behaviors that forensic mental health professionals are qualified to evaluate. Grisso's model emphasizes the use of empirically based data whenever possible, rather than relying solely on observations and clinical impressions. Findings of the FMHA should then be interpreted in terms of the degree to which the person's functional abilities are congruent with those required under the legal standard: is the specific legal competence demonstrated?

PRINCIPLES, GUIDELINES, AND MAXIMS FOR FMHA

Others have described principles, guidelines, and maxims for FMHA, which will be discussed in the next chapter of this book. Heilbrun (2001) proposed 29 specific principles for conducting FMHA, and Melton et al. (2007) also offered broad principles applicable to forensic assessment. Simon and Gold, in an edited volume focusing largely on forensic psychiatry, provided practice guidelines contributed by the author(s) of each chapter. Brodsky (1991, 1999, 2004) has described maxims for expert testimony that focus on expert testimony, much as these other authors have focused on the evaluation and reporting aspects of FMHA. Each of these, to be discussed in detail in the fourth chapter, provides theoretical contributions to a best-practice standard.

Scientific Knowledge Promoting Accurate Observation and Measurement

The methods used by forensic mental health experts in conducting a range of court-related evaluations have been reviewed by a number of researchers (Borum & Grisso, 1995; Heilbrun & Collins, 1995; Horvath, Logan, & Walker, 2002; Nicholson & Norwood, 2000; Otto & Heilbrun, 2002; Ryba, Cooper, & Zapf, 2003; Skeem & Golding, 1998). These studies have reported inconsistency in the quality of forensic assessment practice in general. In addition, there has been an increasing focus on evidence-based practice over the last decade, including approaches to psychotherapy and assessment. For example, Messer (2004) has emphasized the need for empirically supported treatment, and others (Barlow, 2005; Norcross, Beutler, & Levant, 2006; Reed, Kihlstrom, & Messer, 2006) have called for scientifically based therapy *and* the use of assessment instruments with established reliabilities and validities. Barlow (2005) recommended that evaluation strategies be based upon psychometrically sound measures, established by the "best evidence available." Norcross et al. (2006) have argued against relying only on clinical observations and judgment, anecdotal evidence, and customer-satisfaction ratings, emphasizing instead the importance of using assessment tools that have been empirically validated.

ASSESSMENT STRATEGIES FOR FMHA

In FMHA, experts are asked to evaluate behavior related to specific psycholegal competencies. The focus of such evaluations is typically not limited to describing relevant thinking, feelings, symptoms and behavior, or measuring an individual's intellectual functioning. Rather, these highly specific evaluations require assessment strategies developed specifically for FMHA. Certain traditional psychological assessment techniques may be of some value in explaining why a defendant is or is not legally competent. However, other sources of information (including specialized forensic assessment instruments, when available, as well as interviews with the defendant and collaterals, and review of records) also provide important data that are sometimes even more directly relevant to the psycholegal referral question.

For example, in assessing fitness for trial, experts may rely on multiple sources of data, including interviews with the defendant (on such issues as his understanding of the charges against him, his grasp of the role of court personnel and their function as it relates to his case, his relationship with his attorney); a review of the records (e.g., police reports, jail and forensic unit progress notes); interviews with third parties (e.g., treating professional staff, the defendant's attorney); results of forensic assessment instruments (e.g., MacCAT-CA, ECST-R); and findings based on forensically relevant instruments (e.g., SIRS, VIP). Information based on these sources of data provides data of *direct* relevance to the legal referral question(s) (Does the defendant have the necessary capacities to be considered competent to stand trial? Is the defendant feigning symptoms or deficits that would lead to a finding of trial incompetence?). If a traditional test such as the WAIS-III is administered, it will provide information about some capacities (e.g., vocabulary, verbal reasoning, information processing) that is important in describing certain deficits that may interfere with the person's functional capacities to understand charges and assist counsel in her defense. It would not, however, provide a direct measure of functional capacities in the way that a relevant, specialized forensic assessment instrument (FAI) would.

In addition, FMHA (particularly in criminal areas) is conducted on individuals from diverse backgrounds, often populations either not represented or underrepresented in the norms of the instruments employed. Lally (2003), in a survey of experts who were board certified in forensic psychology (ABPP) identified differing views on how to handle the problem of measures that are insufficiently normed on criminal justice populations, and (more generally) on the acceptability (consistent with Frye) of particular psychological tests in FMHA. Participants were asked to rate a number of assessment instruments for acceptability in six areas of forensic practice: trial competence, mental state at the time of the offense, violence risk assessment, sexual violence risk assessment, waiver of *Miranda* rights, and malingering.

Lally concluded that projective techniques were generally rated as unacceptable (especially the use of projective drawings) and that no "general acceptance" standard (consistent with *Frye*) emerged for any particular test because of the lack of agreement on the acceptability of these instruments.

IMPORTANCE OF BEST-PRACTICE STANDARDS

Although FMHA should draw upon scientific knowledge to provide a reliable basis for the observation and selection of methods, establishing a basis for scientifically driven FMHA is challenging. It is even more complex when one considers the importance of specialized forensic assessment instruments and the diversity of the populations being evaluated. A best-practice standard must provide guidance on acceptable methods. In considering such standards, practicing forensic mental health professionals should be familiar with the validity and reliability of the tests and instruments they are considering when planning an assessment strategy. They would need to justify the use of any measure when used with populations not adequately represented in the standardization sample. Experts must also be familiar with the test manuals that contain information on norms, reliability, and validity. Grisso (1986a, 2003) has reviewed a range of forensic assessment instruments in terms of their scientific support. Experts should be well aware of the forensic relevance, applications, and limitations of such measures. Because the issue of response style is an important consideration in FMHA, experts should also be well versed in the scientific properties of tests commonly used to address this critical issue (Rogers, 1997, 2003). Similarly, because third party information is a source of the data upon which opinions are based, forensic mental health professionals should be aware of the value of these sources (Heilbrun, Warren, & Picarello, 2007; Otto, Slobogin, & Greenberg, 2003).

Science Providing Support for FMHA Data Interpretation

To increase the empirical basis for interpretation of data, forensic mental health professions are increasingly incorporating base rates into their evaluations. For example, Monahan reviewed the use of actuarial instruments in conducting assessments for violence risk

(2003). He reported, "The general superiority of statistical over clinical risk assessment in the behavioral sciences has been known for almost a half century . . . (p. 531)." Similarly, Conroy (2003) described problems associated with the clinical prediction of sexual violence risk, concluding, "actuarial approaches are generally more accurate than clinical prediction" (p. 469). In the course of forensic evaluation, however, both nomothetic (group-based) and idiographic (single case) data must be considered (Heilbrun, 2001; Heilbrun et al., 2004). Nomothetic data include norm-referenced instruments and specialized tests, and a consideration of base rates used to compare the litigant to those in relevant known groups. Ideographic data focus on information specific to the individual and to the unique circumstances of the case, comparing that person's characteristics in the specific situation in question to the individual's characteristics at other times. The appropriate use of nomothetic and ideographic evidence contributes to the evaluation's thoroughness and credibility.

The use of specialized forensic assessment instruments (FAIs) with established reliability and validity contributes to the use of empirically based measures when collecting and interpreting FMHA data. A best-practice standard should include the use of such instruments when available and applicable, to increase the comprehensiveness and strengthen the empirical base of the resulting opinions. However, even empirically validated instruments can be misused when interpreted in forensic contexts (DeMatteo & Edens, 2006; Edens, 2001; Skeem, Golding, Cohn, & Berge, 1998), so care must be taken to ensure their appropriate application to the individual and the specifics of the case.

Professional Ethics Contributing to Best-Practice Standards

In seeking to balance such competing influences, forensic mental health professionals seek guidance from their respective codes of ethical conduct. The American Psychological Association's *Ethical Principles of Psychologists and Code of Conduct (Ethics Code)* (APA, 2002a) is written to apply to *all* areas of psychology. Principles are written broadly, to be applicable across a wide range of psychological settings. Consequently, when a psychologist encounters a conflict in a specialized area of practice, the breadth of the applicable principles may offer (limited) specific guidance to the practitioner. For that reason, the American Psychological Association has endorsed a number of guidelines that are more specific to specialty areas. Guidelines include those addressing such legal topics as child custody assessments (APA, 1994), evaluations in child protective matters (APA Committee on Professional Practice and Standards, 1998), and record-keeping (APA, 2007). These guidelines do *not* represent enforceable ethical standards, as are contained in the *Ethics Code*. However, psychology ethics committees on the national and state levels frequently employ them to interpret the broader *Ethics Code*.

In addition to the guidelines endorsed by American Psychological Association, the *Specialty Guidelines for Forensic Psychologists* (*Specialty Guidelines*), published in 1991, serve as a major source of ethics information for forensic psychologists. This document, authored by a committee composed of members from the American Board of Forensic Psychology (ABFP: the forensic certification board of the American Board of Professional Psychology) and the American Psychology-Law Society (AP-LS, Division 41 of APA), represents an aspirational model for forensic psychology practice. Like other ethical guidelines that are separate from the *Ethics Code,* this document is *not* an enforceable code, but it may be used by ethics committees to interpret the *Ethics Code*.

The American Psychiatric Association's *Principles of Medical Ethics with Annotation Especially Applicable to Psychiatry* (American Psychiatric Association, 2001) provides ethical standards that all psychiatric practitioners are expected to follow. However, because this code of conduct is generic, its applicability to forensic psychiatric practice is limited. The American Academy of Psychiatry and the Law (2005) has provided a more specific set of ethical guidelines: *Ethics Guidelines for the Practice of Forensic Psychiatry (Ethics Guidelines)*. These guidelines address four major areas: confidentiality, consent, honesty and striving for objectivity, and qualifications of examiners.

Ethics codes are important in the mental health field. They address risk management issues, protect the civil rights of clients, and clarify the standards of practice for mental health professionals. By adhering to ethical requirements related to confidentiality, informed consent, release of records, and the requirement that mental health professionals be aware of biases that might affect their expert opinions, professionals engage in practice that respects the rights of litigants while providing better information to courts. In setting standards of conduct for mental health professionals, ethics codes help define how the "reasonable prudent professional" should practice. As such, these codes of ethics represent a major source of authority in the development of standards of practice for conducting FMHA.

Professional Ethics Providing Guidance for FMHA Practice

There are marked differences between the role of treating mental health professionals and that of forensic mental health experts. Among the areas in which conflicts may occur are those created by differences between these roles: identifying the "client," the nature of the professional relationship with the client, the nature of confidentiality, demographics of the population of "clients" in forensic cases, competence of the expert, and trust in the client. These areas in which potential conflict and role dilemmas may arise have been discussed in detail during the last decade (Appelbaum, 1997; Appelbaum & Gutheil, 2007; Greenberg & Shuman, 1997; Goldstein, 2003a; Lipsitt, 2003; Rosner, 2003; Weissman & DeBow, 2003). Such conflicts and their ethical resolutions may be addressed either by the forensic mental health professional's code of ethics or in other publications viewed as authoritative in the field. The representative areas of conflict described as follows are considered from the framework of the *Ethical Principles of Psychologists and Code of Conduct (Ethics Code)*, the *Specialty Guidelines for Forensic Psychologists (Specialty Guidelines)*, and the *Ethics Guidelines for the Practice of Forensic Psychiatry (Ethics Guidelines)*.

COMPETENCE

The *Ethics Code* (2002a, Section 2.01) states that competence to practice within one's boundaries of expertise includes a consideration of "education, training, supervised experience, consultation, study, or professional experience." The *Specialty Guidelines* cautions that those practicing in the forensic arena should possess a "fundamental and reasonable level of knowledge and understanding of the legal and professional standards, which govern their participation as experts in the legal proceedings." As such, forensic psychologists must understand the constitutional rights of those they are evaluating, applicable rules of evidence, the nature of expert testimony, and the relevant statutes and case law related to the psycholegal question under consideration. The *Specialty Guidelines* also recognizes that there are no generic experts. Specific expertise must be demonstrated for the particular legal competency in question, and practice should be limited to those legal areas and questions about which they "have specific knowledge, skill, experience, and education." In addition, familiarity with such factors as the examinee's "age, gender, gender identity, race, ethnicity, culture, national origin, religion, sexual orientation, disability, language, or socioeconomic level" is required, as well as competence in the techniques employed in conducting assessment (e.g., psychological tests and specialized forensic assessment instruments). Consistent with this, the *Ethics Guidelines* notes that expertise in the practice of forensic psychiatry should be claimed only in areas in which the psychiatrist has the requisite knowledge, skills, training, and experience. Areas that may require additional expertise, such as the evaluation of children or those from another culture, should not be claimed as areas of qualification unless the psychiatrist has particular expertise in the particular area as well.

WELFARE OF OTHERS

The *Ethics Code* (Section 3.04) requires that all psychologists "take reasonable steps to avoid harming their patients/clients, students . . . and others with whom they work, and to minimize harm where it is foreseen and unavoidable." Multiple relationships that might reasonably interfere with objectivity or effectiveness of professional performance must be avoided. The *Specialty Guidelines* elaborates on these and other potential problems:

- Fee arrangements and prior relationships with parties in a case must be discussed in advance;
- Cases must never be accepted on a contingency fee basis;
- With the exception of a psychological practice in a small community or small hospital, the dual role of treating

psychologist and forensic expert should be avoided;
even within small communities or hospitals, such a dual
role is to be avoided whenever possible;

- Informed consent, when required, must be obtained,
  using language likely to be understood by the person to
  be evaluated;

- When employed by an agency or organization, forensic
  psychologists should inform the examinee about the
  expert's relationship to the agency, the probable uses of
  the information obtained, who will have access to the
  records, and who the client is (Monahan, 1980);

- If an examinee is unable or unwilling to grant informed
  consent when it is required, the assessment should be
  postponed. The individual's attorney should be con-
  sulted before further contact with the examinee is made.

The *Ethics Guidelines* does not have a specific section on the welfare of the individual being evaluated. However, some considerations in
this area are addressed in the section on consent. It indicates that forensic psychiatrists should obtain the informed consent of the evaluee
when "necessary and feasible," and that individuals who are not able to
give consent should be dealt with according to applicable jurisdictional
law. It is clear that this section does not require informed consent for
all forensic psychiatric evaluations; in certain instances (e.g., court-
ordered evaluations), the psychiatrist should provide a notification of
purpose but not seek either consent or assent. It precludes the evaluation of individuals not represented by counsel when the evaluation is
not court-ordered and the individual is charged with, under investigation for, or being interrogated concerning criminal acts.

Confidentiality and Privacy

Although its breach is not a frequent source of ethics complaints
(APA, 2005), confidentiality is the most often cited ethical concern of
psychologists (Pope & Vetter, 1992). The *Ethics Code* (Section 4.01)
indicates that psychologists "have a primary obligation and take reasonable precautions to protect confidential information . . . recognizing that the extent and limits of confidentiality may be regulated by

law or established by institutional rules or professional or scientific relationship." The limits of confidentiality must be discussed with clients, and only information relevant "to the purpose for which the communication is made [should be included]" (Section 4.04). Therefore, intrusions on the examinee's right to privacy should be minimized. The code (Section 4.05) also cautions that psychologists "should disclose confidential information without the consent of the individual only as mandated by law, or where permitted by law for a valid purpose."

The *Specialty Guidelines* emphasizes the need to avoid revealing information about an individual when such information is not directly relevant to the legal purpose of the evaluation. Specially, no information or statements provided by a defendant in a criminal case should be used to address any legal issue "except on the issue respecting mental condition on which the defendant has introduced testimony." Forensic psychologists should report information only relevant to the legal issue for which they were retained, and for which the individual has provided informed consent. The following, more specific elaboration is provided in the *Specialty Guidelines:*

- Anonymous sources of information as a basis for a forensic opinion should be avoided;

- Unless court ordered, information should be disclosed only with appropriate consent;

- All identifying data about an individual should be disguised in writing, teaching and supervision.

According to the *Ethics Guidelines,* respect for the individual's right of privacy and the maintenance of confidentiality are major concerns in conducting forensic psychiatric evaluations. Confidentiality should be maintained to the extent possible under the legal circumstances. The anticipated limitations to confidentiality should not only be described to the evaluee, but to collateral sources as well.

PUBLIC STATEMENTS, RECORD KEEPING, AND FEES
The *Ethics Code* (Section 6.02) indicates that all psychologists are expected to "maintain confidentiality in creating, storing, accessing, transferring, and disposing of records under their control. . . ." The

APA *Record Keeping Guidelines* (2007) provides psychologists with a general framework regarding the maintenance and retention of records, both written and electronic. These aspiration guidelines are meant to assist psychologists in making decisions concerning how detailed records should be, how long records should be maintained and how to dispose of them, and on related questions involving confidentiality and security. (These issues are also addressed by the *Ethics Code* and the *Specialty Guidelines*). This document emphasizes the aspirational intent of these guidelines, and decisions about these issues are left to psychologists, who "should be familiar with legal and ethical requirements for record keeping in their specific professional contexts and jurisdictions" (p. 993). As such, jurisdictional laws supersede these guidelines. Some contexts require more detailed record keeping, and the psychologist should balance "client care with legal and ethical requirements and risks" (p. 995). Work performed in a psycholegal context calls for more detailed records because of the expectation that the results of the FMHA will be used in legal proceedings, and the records relied upon to explain and support the opinions reached by the psychologist. Records in forensic contexts may also be relevant at a future time, unrelated to the initial reason for the referral. For example, an evaluee in a criminal case may win an appeal and be granted a new trial, in which records and testimony are again needed.

The *Record Keeping Guidelines* addresses three conflicts that frequently arise when psychologists are employed by or conduct FMHA for agencies and other organizations. Issues may be related to the policies of the organization versus the ethics of the profession, who "owns" the records, and who has access to these documents. In each of these instances, the guidelines suggest that psychologists attempt to resolve these conflicts and, if unsuccessful, strive to follow the *Ethics Code* and the *Record Keeping Guidelines*. The guidelines recommend that psychologists consider maintaining all records "until seven years after the last date of service for adults or until three years after a minor reaches the age of majority, whichever is last" (p. 999). Consistent with the guidelines' contextual perspective, we recommend that in forensic contexts, psychologists should consider retaining full records for a longer period of time.

The *Specialty Guidelines* notes that forensic evaluations have a higher standard for documentation than do clinical assessments and treatment. Forensic psychology requires "the best documentation possible," as those in forensic mental health practice should anticipate that their work might be used in litigation. When conducting FMHA, therefore, detailed notes should be taken during interviews and relied upon in forming opinions, writing reports, and offering expert testimony. These records document the substance of the interviews and provide the data upon which opinions are based. The *Specialty Guidelines* also indicates that forensic psychologists should avoid offering out of court statements to third parties, including the media, unless "there is a strong justification to do so." Such statements may unnecessarily infringe on an examinee's privacy. Unless an evaluator is authorized to speak about a case outside the context of the standard communication associated with that case (e.g., report, deposition, expert testimony), then *Ethics Code* standards and the guidelines contained in the *Specialty Guidelines* regarding confidentiality may be violated. In addition, out of court statements can serve as a basis for cross-examination, and may raise questions about the forensic mental health expert's credibility.

Although public statements are not addressed directly by the *Ethics Guidelines*, there is the continuing assumption that the forensic psychiatrist will maintain confidence of relevant information except as dictated by the legal context of the evaluation. In addition, the evaluee could consent to the release of such information in a public way, but this would necessitate fully informed consent. Of course, this would not preclude public statements being made in such a way as to avoid revealing case-specific information. For instance, a forensic psychiatrist involved in a high profile case in which the defendant asserted an insanity defense might comment on the insanity defense, its purpose and how it was evaluated, and how individuals acquitted by reason of insanity are treated—but decline to provide information or opinions regarding the defendant that he has evaluated in this particular case.

ASSESSMENT

Section 9.01 of the *Ethics Code* advises all psychologists that "forensic testimony [must rely] on information and techniques sufficient to substantiate their findings." Opinions should be offered only when there has been an examination of the individual "adequate to support their statements or conclusions." If it is not possible to conduct a face-to-face interview with the litigant, records should document the efforts made to schedule such a session and "clarify the probable impact of their limited information on the reliability and validity of their opinions, and appropriately limit the nature and extent of their conclusions or recommendations."

Testing data frequently serve as an additional source of information upon which FMHA opinions are based. The *Ethics Code* (Section 9.02) requires that all psychologists use testing instruments "in a manner and for the purposes that are appropriate in light of the research." Test instruments should have reliability and validity that "have been established for use with members of the population being tested." If reliability and validity have *not* been established for a specific population or cultural group, the psychologist must describe the strengths and limitations of the results obtained. Similarly, testing should be conducted in language appropriate for the individual's "language preference and competence, unless the use of an alternative language is relevant to the assessment issue." For example, in the context of a forensic assessment to evaluate a defendant's competence to waive *Miranda* rights, English may be the appropriate language to use with the examinee if the rights were read to or by the defendant in English.

Raw testing data (e.g., actual test stimuli and questions, test manuals, the examinee's answers, and test scores) may be misused by non-psychologists. Consequently, both the *Ethics Code* and the *Specialty Guidelines* contain cautions about the release of raw data to those who are not trained to interpret them. The *Ethics Code* (Section 9.04) states that raw test data are released "only as required by law or court order" in the absence of a signed release by the examinee. In addition, all psychologists make reasonable efforts to maintain test integrity and security, consistent with the law's requirements.

The *Specialty Guidelines* indicates that the disclosure of information to non-psychologists based upon psychological testing is made only when every effort has been taken "to ensure that test security has been maintained and access to information is restricted to individuals with a legitimate and professional interest in the data." When such information is sent to non-psychologists, the *Specialty Guidelines* advises "the forensic psychologist [to take] . . . reasonable steps to ensure that the receiving party is informed that raw scores must be interpreted by a qualified professional in order to provide reliable and valid information."

Many objective personality tests, such as the MMPI-2, the MCMI-III and the PAI, can be computer-scored and interpreted. In selecting scoring services to perform this function, the *Specialty Guidelines* states that services should be selected "on the basis of evidence of validity of the program and procedures." Although these tests may be scored and independently interpreted, forensic psychologists continue to "retain responsibility for the appropriate application, interpretation, and use of assessment instruments." The ultimate responsibility for test security, knowledge about the test, correct administration and scoring, and interpretation rests with the psychologist. Scores and test interpretations printed from a computer program are *not* a substitute for specific knowledge about and correct use of a test.

The question of the importance of a personal interview is addressed by the *Ethics Guidelines*. Honesty, objectivity, and the adequacy of the clinical evaluation, it is noted, may be questioned if the expert offers an opinion without a personal examination. Some evaluations, such as record reviews, do not require such personal contacts. In other instances, if it is not feasible to conduct a personal examination (but there has been reasonable effort to do so), the psychiatrist may render an opinion based on other information. When doing so, however, the psychiatrist must both observe that no personal examination was conducted and note any limitations that may have resulted from the absence of such an interview.

ULTIMATE OPINION TESTIMONY

The *Ethics Code* indicates that psychologists:

- Should provide services only within their boundaries of expertise (Section 2.01),
- Offer statements or opinions only when there are sufficient data to support their findings (Section 9.01),

- Use assessment techniques only for those "purposes that are appropriate in light of the research on or evidence of the usefulness and proper application of the techniques" (Section 9.02).

An examination of these standards, when applied to FMHA, provides some support for the argument against the forensic psychologist's answering the ultimate legal question. If the focus of the FMHA is on the functional legal criteria, then psychologists can restrict their assessment to domains that are scientific and clinical—and avoid the political, moral, and community value-laden influences that invariably affect the determination of the legal issue. Psychologists do not have particular expertise in values, as they do in scientific and clinical aspects of mental health, and so should not count values as part of their "forensic expertise." Nor should they allow attorneys to broaden the scope of their opinion (to include the ultimate legal issue) if they do not consider this as part of their opinion. In fairness, however, it should be added that Section 2.01 certainly does not make it clear that ultimate issue conclusions and testimony are to be avoided. What the forensic psychologist guided by the *Ethics Code* must consider is whether she regards ultimate issue conclusions as within her boundaries of expertise—and whether she has "sufficient data" to support her findings and conclusion on this issue.

Are FMHA techniques appropriate for answering the ultimate legal question? Consider the relevant research or evidence for proper application and usefulness of these techniques. It is noteworthy that many of the specialized forensic assessment instruments (see Grisso, 1986, 2003) have been developed and validated using functional legal criteria (e.g., understanding of charges and capacity to assist counsel) rather than ultimate legal issues (e.g., competence to stand trial). But it is also true that in some jurisdictions, the failure to provide such an answer would result in the exclusion of the FMHA entirely. Much of the argument against providing an ultimate legal opinion is eliminated if the forensic clinician is thorough, provides data clearly, and describes the reasoning link between such data and conclusions. This is described more clearly in the *Specialty Guidelines.*

The *Specialty Guidelines* indicates that forensic psychologists should communicate "in ways that will promote understanding and avoid deception." Presenting an ultimate opinion in a report or testimony has the potential to misrepresent or over-interpret the results of FMHA, thereby violating this caution. In addition, the *Specialty Guidelines* indicates that forensic psychologists:

- Must present their findings "in a manner consistent with professional and legal standards,"

- Have, in their public statements, "a special responsibility for fairness and accuracy," and

- In offering expert evidence, must be "aware that their own professional observations, inferences and conclusions must be distinguished from legal facts, opinions and conclusions."

The *Ethics Guidelines* does not address the question of ultimate legal opinions. In the section on honesty and striving for objectivity, however, it does indicate that forensic psychiatrists should distinguish, as much as possible, between verified and unverified information, and among clinical "facts," "inferences," and "impressions." Perhaps the most straightforward way to distinguish clinical facts and inferences from moral values is to refrain from answering the ultimate legal question as part of the FMHA. But there *is* consensus that the forensic clinician should carefully separate data, reasoning, and conclusions in this process. If this is done, then it is less important whether the ultimate legal question is answered.

Professional Ethics Affecting the Regulation of FMHA Practice

Codes of ethics and specialized forensic guidelines have an indirect influence on regulating the practice of forensic mental health professionals. Although ethics codes have no legal authority, violations of such ethical standards can result in referrals to state ethics committees or boards of psychology. Adjudication by the licensing board can result in suspension or loss of license under applicable administrative law.

Ethics codes identify the competency requirements to practice in specific forensic areas and the ways in which expertise is identified.

Other documents, such as the *Specialty Guidelines,* describe the extent of knowledge an expert should possess in order to practice ethically ("a fundamental and reasonable degree of knowledge" of the legal system, statutes and case law that influence FMHA, rules of evidence, and the legal rights of individuals who are evaluated). In addition to defining the boundaries of practice, codes of ethics require forensic mental health practitioners to be well versed in the tests and instruments they use in gathering forensic data, and the applicability of those measures to the litigant. Violations of these and other ethical principles do not result in loss of licensure. However, some states and provinces have adopted ethics codes as part of their own regulatory requirements. These bodies have the authority to legally regulate the practice of FMHA through requiring supervision, restricting practice, or suspending or eliminating licensure.

Professional Practice Contributing to Best-Practice Standards

Centers for specialized training (e.g., the Institute of Law, Psychiatry, and Public Policy, University of Virginia; the Center for Forensic Psychiatry, Ypsilanti, Michigan; Federal Bureau of Prisons, Springfield, Missouri; University of Massachusetts Medical School, Worcester, Massachusetts) and recognized board certification organizations, combined with the professional practice literature, serve as a fourth source of authority when addressing the components of best-practice standards. Each of these will be discussed in this section.

Professional Organizations Guiding FMHA Practice

Ethics codes promulgated by the American Psychological Association and the American Psychiatric Association establish broad principles regarding competence in a specific area of practice. Professional organizations help define, albeit generally, the minimum requirements for specialization. The *Specialty Guidelines* applies these broader principles to the more specific practice of FMHA. Although professional organizations cannot remove a mental health professional's license to practice, those conducting FMHA "are answerable to their professional organization (as well as to state boards in which they hold licenses) for complaints of ethical misconduct" (Goldstein, 2003b, p. 6).

The substantial growth in professional organizations that focus on the intersection of the law and psychology, such as the American Psychology-Law Society (AP-LS), the American Board of Forensic Psychology, and American Academy of Psychiatry and Law, has contributed to the development and dissemination of forensic research, scientific knowledge, ethics, and practice expertise. Several commentators (e.g., Heilbrun et al., in press; Otto & Heilbrun, 2002) have suggested that formal practice guidelines provided by professional organizations can make an important contribution to establishing a standard of practice. Consistent with this, Wettstein (2005), in a discussion on improving the quality of forensic evaluations, calls for establishing quality guidelines and standards, which can then be applied through peer review, continuing education, and cross-examination in testimony regarding the expert's participation in such activities.

PRACTICE GUIDELINES FOR FORENSIC SUB-SPECIALTIES
With new areas for FMHA emerging and the practice of forensic psychology and psychiatry expanding (Goldstein, 2007), professional organizations will need to provide ethical and practice guidelines for forensic sub-specialties. Some important steps have already been taken in this regard. The American Academy of Psychiatry and Law is currently working to develop practice guidelines for evaluations on different legal questions. Published guidelines to date include those on sanity at the time of the offense (American Academy of Psychiatry and Law, 2002) and competence to stand trial (Mossman et al., 2007).

The American Academy of Child and Adolescent Psychiatry has also published a series of "practice parameters" for psychiatric evaluation in various areas. These include the assessment of child custody (1997), possible physical or sexual abuse (1997), conduct disorder (1997), posttraumatic stress disorder (1998), and sexual abuse of others (1999),

Some direction has also been provided by other American Psychological Association divisions through the development of guidelines for the use of personnel selection procedures (Society for Industrial and Organizational Psychology, 2003), the provision of

services to those with developmental disabilities and mental retardation (www.apa.org/divisions/div33/effectivetreatment.html), and
by the American Psychological Association itself on multicultural education, research, and practice (American Psychological Association,
2002b). In addition, the *Guidelines for Child Custody Evaluations in
Divorce Proceedings* (APA, 1994) and the *Guidelines for Psychological
Evaluations in Child Protection Matters* (APA, 1999) are relevant to
the forensic assessment of children and adolescents in these areas. The
revision of the 1991 *Specialty Guidelines for Forensic Psychologists* is
well underway at the time this is being written, and should be published in the *American Psychologist* when it is complete.

Finally, the Association of Family and Conciliation Courts
(undated, later 2006) has disseminated model standards of practice
for child custody evaluations. It is thus apparent that both psychiatry
and psychology have been active in the development of aspirational
descriptions of the practice of various aspects of forensic mental
health assessment during the last two decades, particularly during the
1997–2007 decade. The details of these various guidelines will be
covered in the books in this series on each of the respective topics.
However, it is important to note that there have been ongoing efforts
to develop and refine these guidelines made by different professional
organizations, reflecting their views on aspirational practice.

Centers for Specialized Training Guiding FMHA Practice

One way to examine the elements that contribute to FMHA is to consider what is taught to those seeking to become experts or to those
looking to expand their practice into relatively new areas. The common ground across various programs can help inform the development of a best-practice standard. Training in FMHA occurs at a
number of levels. These include graduate programs, internships, postdoctoral fellowships, and continuing professional education.

GRADUATE PROGRAMS

As of July 2007, ten universities and colleges offered Master of Arts
degrees in forensic psychology, according to the AP-LS website
(www.ap-ls.org). At the doctoral level, almost all of the 17 universities

providing doctoral-level specialty training in forensic psychology do so with a "forensic concentration" as part of a doctoral program in clinical or counseling psychology. In addition, a number of programs offer joint degrees in law (J.D.) and psychology (Ph.D. or Psy.D.), and may provide training in forensic psychology as part of this interdisciplinary work. (The AP-LS website is updated on a regular basis, so the reader should consult this website for a current listing.)

Universities resist offering doctoral degrees in forensic psychology because of limitations imposed on potential practitioners by state or provincial licensing laws. (Other reasons for declining to offer doctoral degrees in forensic psychology include the potential for premature specialization and the current disinclination of the American Psychological Association to accredit applied doctoral training programs in areas other than clinical, counseling, and school psychology.) Specifically, laws that regulate the practice of psychology are written to address the training and course requirements of clinical or counseling psychologists. A range of clinical psychology courses is required to meet licensure regulations—because of the large number of specific clinical courses needed to sit for the licensing examination, students who might otherwise enroll in a "purely" forensic program could not meet a jurisdiction's licensing requirements.

An examination of the core forensic course curriculum and course syllabi of doctoral and joint degree programs could serve as a source of authority as to what constitutes a best-practice standard in FMHA.

LEVELS OF SPECIALTY TRAINING

Three levels of specialty training of forensic mental health practitioners were delineated at the National Invitational Conference on Education and Training in Law and Psychology, held at the Villanova Law School in 1995 (Bersoff, Goodman-Delahunty, Grisso, Hans, Poythress, & Roesch, 1997). The first level of training, *the legally informed clinician,* requires that psychologists receive basic legal education and some forensic content in doctoral-level clinical courses, particularly those focusing on assessment and ethics. It has been reasoned that *"all* clinicians, not only those who specialize in forensic psychology, need to be aware of certain aspects of the law that may impact their practice" (Packer & Borum, 2003, p. 25).

At the intermediate level, *proficiency in forensic psychology,* are those who have received training at "general professional programs, with an emphasis on forensics" (Bersoff et al., 1999, p. 1309). For those who already hold doctoral degrees, training could occur in postdoctoral programs or through continuing education offerings. At this level, in addition to course work, there would be a requirement for supervised experience in forensic settings such as jails, forensic hospitals, or court clinics. Training in presenting expert testimony and consulting with attorneys would be offered, and graduate students would typically be expected to complete dissertations on forensic topics. Packer and Borum (2003) observed that the goal of training at this level is to establish competency in one or more areas of forensic practice as a supplement to traditional clinical work.

At the highest level—*specialization in forensic psychology*—the training involves completing a program "dedicated to producing forensic psychologists . . . [through] an integrated, carefully developed sequence of training with an identifiable, experienced forensic faculty with recognized credentials" (Bersoff, et al., 1999, p. 1306). This level of training includes didactic training with a detailed study of law, and intensive supervised experience in evaluating a variety of psycholegal issues involving litigants from diverse backgrounds (Packer & Borum, 2003). It would be expected that those trained at this level would ultimately complete a postdoctoral fellowship and earn American Board of Professional Psychology (ABPP) board certification in forensic psychology. This is not to imply that others, trained at a non-specialist level, could not attain ABPP board certification in forensic psychology. However, it is likely that additional training and supervised experience would be needed if someone trained at the *legally informed* or *proficiency* levels sought such board certification.

INTERNSHIPS AND POSTDOCTORAL FELLOWSHIPS

Doctoral internships offer a route for graduate students to acquire specific knowledge and training in FMHA. Internship training in FMHA may occur in prison settings, forensic hospitals, court clinics, or other clinical settings in which this kind of assessment is conducted. An analysis of what is taught in such settings, including the methodology used to conduct specific FMHA, may shed light on a best-practice standard for FMHA.

Training in FMHA for those who have completed a doctorate in psychology usually occurs via postdoctoral fellowships or as the result of participating in continuing education programs offered by an APA-approved sponsor. A limited number (approximately 11) of postdoctoral fellowships in forensic psychology exist (Packer & Borum, 2003). Typically such programs involve a single year of training, with some offering a second year. Packer and Borum (2003) present a sample curriculum for a postdoctoral fellowship in forensic psychology, discussing the texts and substance that postdoctoral fellows typically learn during a training year. For psychiatrists seeking to obtain specialty training in forensic psychiatry, there are a number of forensic fellowships available in the United States (see www.aapl.com). The path to forensic specialization in forensic psychiatry also includes board certification through the American Board of Psychiatry and Neurology ("with Added Qualifications in Forensic Psychiatry").

CONTINUING EDUCATION PROGRAMS

There are many continuing education programs dedicated to presenting relevant research, case law, ethics, and methods to mental health professionals. These include seminars presented by the American Psychology-Law Society and the American Academy of Forensic Psychology (AAFP). AAFP, an affiliate of the American Board of Forensic Psychology (ABFP), has been an APA-approved sponsor for over 25 years. Typically, a series of workshops is presented at a specific location in the United States and Canada six or seven times a year, most taught by individuals who are either board certified in forensic psychology (ABPP), or not board certified but nonetheless recognized experts in specific areas of forensic research or practice. The content of these presentations and an analysis of the workshop materials can serve to inform a best-practice standard, which could incorporate the books and other materials used in this series (many of which are authored or coauthored by AAFP workshop presenters). In forensic psychiatry, the American Academy of Psychiatry and the Law offers a three-day intensive training course specifically for individuals (already board certified in general psychiatry) who seek subspecialty board certification in forensic psychiatry. This training includes case law, ethics, research, and practice literature that are all directly relevant to the practice of forensic psychiatry at a highly specialized level.

Board Certification Guiding FMHA Practice

The American Board of Professional Psychology confers board certification in forensic psychology on those who meet the credentialing requirements of its member board, the American Board of Forensic Psychology. ABPP, established in 1947, is the oldest and most rigorous of the organizations offering board certification in forensic psychology; it also provides certification in 12 other specialties in applied psychology (Marczyk, DeMatteo, Kutinsky, & Heilbrun, 2007). Successful candidates for forensic board certification must possess an earned doctoral degree from an APA-approved program (or one that meets APA criteria), maintain an active license as a psychologist, and have completed a minimum of 100 hours of APA-approved continuing education and face-to-face supervision in forensic psychology as well as 1,000 hours of experience in forensic psychology obtained over a five-year period.

Case law and recommended readings that applicants should know for both the written and oral examinations are found on the ABFP website (www.abfp.com). A review of the texts, chapters, published research, and case law appearing there reflects the core body of knowledge required of those who would demonstrate a high degree of specialization in forensic psychology in seeking to satisfy ABPP standards for forensic psychology board certification. Much of the work cited in this book (e.g., Goldstein, 2003a; Grisso, 2003; Heilbrun, 2001; Melton, Petrila, Poythress & Slobogin, 2007) also appears on this recommended list. This set of readings reflects sources of authority in the field that are relevant for an FMHA best-practice standard, as applicants are examined in areas including law, ethics, testing and assessment, individual rights and liberties, juvenile and family law, personal injury and other civil assessments, criminal competencies, and criminal responsibility.

The American Board of Psychiatry and Neurology awards "Certification in the Subspecialty of Forensic Psychiatry" to psychiatrists who meet rigorous qualification and examination criteria. Applicants must first become board certified from ABPN in general psychiatry. Effective 2001, applicants must also have completed an approved one-year fellowship in forensic psychiatry. Successful candidates must also pass an examination covering areas including the legal regulation of psychiatry, criminal law, civil law, methodology, risk assessment, diagnosis and treatment, and forensic psychiatry practice. In addition to a review course offered by the American Academy of Psychiatry and the Law, a list of required case law is provided for those interested in pursuing forensic psychiatry subspecialty certification (see www.aapl.org). The information presented at AAPL workshops, topics covered by the written examination, and the case law listed on the website contribute to the development of a standard for best practice in FMHA for forensic psychiatrists.

Conclusion

The major sources of authority contributing to the practice of forensic psychology and forensic psychiatry have been considered in this chapter. Law, ethics, science, and professional practice constitute the broad domains into which these sources fall. Although there are certainly disciplinary differences between psychology and psychiatry that are reflected in how these two professions conceptualize, train, and practice in their respective forensic specializations, the common ground appears to greatly outweigh disciplinary differences. One important source of authority—practice literature describing principles, guidelines, and maxims—was discussed only briefly in this chapter. It is to these sources that we will turn our attention in the next chapter.

Principles of Forensic Mental Health Assessment | 4

"**P**rinciples" are constituent parts a larger body (Black, 1983; Heilbrun, 2001). In our present context, they are broad theoretical components of forensic mental health assessment that can be distinguished from more specific, detailed guidelines that may be derived from them. They may inform the development of a standard of practice. However, as a broad consensus of the field concerning acceptable professional behavior, a standard of practice should also be informed by ethics codes, practice guidelines, empirical findings, and broad reviews of the field that do not describe principles.

Are there broad principles of FMHA that serve as a foundation for this kind of specialized assessment? This is a question that has been discussed by psycholegal scholars for about a decade. In this chapter, we will describe the works of Simon and Gold (2004) in offering specific guidelines related for FMHA, and that of Melton and colleagues (1997, 2007); Heilbrun (2001) and colleagues (Heilbrun, DeMatteo & Marczyk, 2004; Heilbrun, Marczyk, & DeMatteo, 2002); and Brodsky (1991, 1999, 2004) in deriving, discussing, and generalizing broad principles of FMHA. These broad discussions will then be integrated later in this chapter to reflect our views about the current status of principles applicable to FMHA.

There are two distinct approaches to considering the process of forensic mental health assessment. The great majority of psycholegal scholars have identified a distinct form of FMHA, as defined by the legal question, and elaborated on the relevant law, ethical contours, supporting data, practice literature, and specialized tools. This is the approach taken by a number of scholars (e.g., Grisso, 1986, 2003; Hess & Weiner, 1999; Melton et al., 1987, 1997, 2007; Weiner & Hess, 1987, 2005) who have written overviews of the field.

There is a different perspective, however, that begins with the assumption that all forms of FMHA share some common foundation. This approach looks for the common elements of FMHA that occur across different kinds of forensic evaluations. Several scholars, for example, have described a "model" on which FMHA is based (see Grisso, 1986, 2003; Morse, 1978). Both Simon and Gold (2004) and Melton et al. (2007) include a description of different kinds of forensic assessment in addition to their discussion of common guidelines and elements. Apparently only Heilbrun (2001) approached this discussion by focusing exclusively on foundational principles of FMHA, but he subsequently expanded it to apply to different forms of FMHA (Heilbrun, DeMatteo & Marczyk, 2004; Heilbrun, Marczyk, & DeMatteo, 2002).

This best-practice series has adopted a similar strategy. We are beginning with the present book, which focuses on foundational aspects of FMHA. Among these foundational aspects are the guidelines and principles discussed in this chapter. Then the series turns to books on specific FMHA topics (see Table 5.1). In this respect, we will use a strategy that has been employed by a number of others who have described both the distinctive and common elements of FMHA. "FMHA best practice," therefore, will be described in terms of both foundational aspects (the present book) and specific elements (the respective series books on particular FMHA topics).

Guidelines: Simon and Gold

Simon & Gold (2004a) provide chapters on a number of different topics within forensic psychiatry.[1] These include broad aspects of the practice of forensic psychiatry, such as "starting a forensic practice," "expert witness" functions, malingering, and violence. They also include specific legal topics under civil litigation (e.g., personal injury, disability) and criminal law (e.g., competence to stand trial, insanity). Each chapter provides "practice guidelines" at the end of the chapters, so the book captures the views of the 27 contributing authors as well as the two editors on applicable guidelines.

---

[1]Forensic psychiatric assessment and forensic psychological assessment are both included under the rubric of *forensic mental health assessment,* so for the sake of convenience we will refer to forensic psychiatric assessment as "FMHA" unless there is something distinctly psychiatric or medical about it.

This edited book offers a useful opportunity to derive guidelines for the practice of forensic psychiatric assessment. The tone of the volume is less normative ("this is how it's usually done") than aspirational ("this is how it ought to be done"), so the guidelines offered by chapter authors at the conclusion of each of the chapters have implications for our discussion of best practice. Most of the guidelines offered in this way can be found in Table 4.1. Chapters have different authors and address distinct topics. Consequently, some of the guidelines are cited by more than one author, and in somewhat different ways.

Looking across chapters and at the different kinds of evaluations for guidelines that recur is one strategy for identifying broader, more principled approaches to FMHA conducted by forensic psychiatrists. The guidelines are cited in the context of the specific chapter's topic, so they are not necessarily intended to apply to FMHA broadly. But in many respects, the guidelines offered by chapter authors in the Simon and Gold volume *are* consistent with the broader FMHA components advanced by Melton and colleagues (1987, 1997, 2007) and by Heilbrun and colleagues (2001, 2002). This may be seen in Table 4.1 on the next page and will be discussed briefly.

Clinical and Forensic Roles

The first guideline (#1 in Table 4.1; Gold, 2004) points to the distinction between clinical and forensic roles, and is also addressed in detail by Melton et al. (2007) (see Table 4.2) and Heilbrun (see Table 4.3). The importance of appropriate training (Guideline #2; Gold, 2004) and specific training in relevant ethical and legal domains (#5; Shuman, 2004) underscores one necessary step in any kind of specialization—the forensic clinician must know enough about the law and about forensic ethics to function effectively in this specialized context.

A number of authors address the issue of dual roles (treating clinician vs. forensic evaluator) in FMHA. Two proffered guidelines reflect straightforward opposition to any form of simultaneous dual agency (#6: "Do not mix therapeutic and forensic roles," Shuman, 2004; #65: "Avoid forensic evaluations of one's own patients," Ash, 2004). A second suggests that dual roles be avoided "whenever possible" (#27, Weinstock & Gold, 2004). A third is more elaborate: "Do not, with some exceptions, serve as expert witness for your own

Table 4.1 | Practice Guidelines for FMHA
(Guidelines from Simon & Gold, 2004, reprinted with
permission from American Psychiatric Publishing Inc.)

1. Be aware of the significant differences between the practice of clinical and forensic psychiatry.

2. Obtain appropriate forensic training to provide the courts with quality expert services.

3. Be prepared for challenges to your professional reputation and opinions, no matter how extensive your clinical experience or forensic skills.

4. Remain humble: the trier of fact ultimately settles the matter in dispute. The expert's testimony is one part of a larger picture, seen in its entirety only by the court.

5. Obtain comprehensive education and training addressing the ethical guidelines and legal rules that govern the practice of forensic psychiatry before providing expert witness services or consultations.

6. Do not mix therapeutic and forensic roles.

7. Provide expert testimony only on questions for which your education, training, and experience provide specialized expertise.

8. Use methods and procedures whose reliability has been tested and proven according to the most demanding standards of the profession.

9. Offer opinions that are based on sufficient, reliable information.

10. Present your findings in a manner that permits the fact finder to follow your analysis.

11. Interact frequently with the legal and business communities.

12. Practice an objective, evidence-based medical model.

13. Embrace technology to improve efficiency.

14. Produce coherent, user-friendly reports.

15. Use clear, written contracts with clients.

16. Provide clear instructions to examinees.

17. Understand the meaning of the expert's role functions in the legal system.

continued

18. Thoroughly review the database, and request missing pieces from the attorney.

19. Derive an opinion supportable by the evidence in the database; this may mean telling the retaining attorney that you cannot support the case. Be morally, financially, and psychologically prepared to turn down a case that has no merit.

20. Strive to overcome bias, or failing this, pass on the case. The overarching principles of honesty and striving for objectivity should govern the process.

21. In gray-zone cases, negotiate with the attorney about the limits and boundaries of the opinion, permitting flexibility but resisting attorney pressures for substantive changes.

22. Do not, with some exceptions, serve as expert witness for your own patients. In rare cases—geographic unavailability of other clinicians or unique training or knowledge—you may be drafted into the expert role, though this may alter the treatment relationship.

23. Accept and prepare for the chaotic time lines of the legal system.

24. Be familiar with the ethical guidelines provided by AAPL, the APA, and other professional organizations as they relate to clinical and forensic practice.

25. As far as possible, consider the ethical aspects of any potential forensic case before agreeing to participate, and attempt to withdraw from any case in which there is pressure to perform an unethical role.

26. Adhere to the ethical principles of honesty and striving for objectivity in all forensic cases.

27. Avoid occupying dual-agency roles whenever possible.

28. Identify the necessity for inclusion or exclusion of psychiatric diagnosis in accordance with the relevant legal statute.

29. Identify the functional capacity directly relevant to the legal issue in question and evaluate functional impairment, if any.

30. Explain the relationship between the diagnosis and the relevant functional capacity. If an unreasonable or invalid inference of

continued

functional impairment is being made on the basis of any given diagnosis, explain the lack of correlation between or incorrect reasoning about the diagnosis and functional capacity in question.

31. Do not substitute the formulation of a DSM diagnosis for a careful forensic evaluation of the relevant functional capacity in question.

32. Avoid forcing sub-syndromal and other psychiatric conditions into catchall NOS diagnoses. This results in the substitution of an imprecise diagnosis for the provision of substantive information about the relationship between symptom severity and functional impairment.

33. Self-monitor case selection.

34. Remain within one's expertise.

35. Obtain comprehensive data from original sources.

36. Perform multiple interviews with evaluee.

37. Obtain corroborative data.

38. Reconcile conflicting data.

39. Offer same opinion regardless of retaining side.

40. Self-monitor pattern of forensic opinions.

41. Fully substantiate basis for forensic opinions.

42. Disclose limitations of forensic opinions.

43. Do not become competitive with opposing experts.

44. Undertake peer review.

45. Clarify issues regarding expertise, conflict of interest, bias, and fees during the initial contact with the attorney to avoid problems in these areas later in the case.

46. Carefully consider attorneys' requests. Comply only with those that do not detrimentally affect the evaluation or compromise ethical or professional integrity.

47. Become familiar with the relevant elements of the legal process such as discovery, deposition, and courtroom testimony. Such familiarity will improve performance and decrease anxiety.

48. Be respectful of colleagues involved in the legal process.

continued

49. Provide and seek mentoring freely. Learning from the experience of others and passing on learned wisdom results in personal and professional growth.

50. Base opinions on a careful review of the records, interviews, and examination of relevant person; knowledge of the relevant medical literature; and your training and experience.

51. Remember that colleagues retained by the opposite side can and will come to different conclusions. Expert testimony on both sides of an adversarial process is intended to assist the trier of fact in understanding both sides of the legal arguments.

52. Base diagnoses, to the extent possible, on objective, rather than subjective, data. This includes observations during the mental status examination and collateral data with such as record review and interviews with family, friends, and associates.

53. Determine the legal issues relevant to the type of litigation and structure the evaluation accordingly.

54. Identify the nature of the evaluation and limitation issues regarding the evaluation at the outset.

55. Attend to and clarify ethical issues regarding confidentiality and agency before beginning the evaluation.

56. Use appropriate psychological and psychophysiological instruments to gather relevant information. Testing should be administered by a qualified and experienced expert, and results should be considered in light of both strengths and limitations of the instruments used.

57. Use all available data from collateral sources, interview, and testing to formulate well-reasoned opinions.

58. Consider malingering in the differential diagnosis, especially in forensic settings.

59. During the initial interview, be on the watch for endorsement of an unusually high number of symptoms that are rare, blatant, absurd, and preposterous and that are non-selectively endorsed.

60. Review collateral data for consistencies or inconsistencies that support or refute malingering.

continued

61. Obtain psychological testing when the clinical and structured interviews result in a suspicion of malingering.

62. Make a diagnosis of malingering on the basis of a thorough assessment that integrates many sources of information.

63. Be clear on the forensic question being asked.

64. Clarify who is requesting evaluation, to whom the report will be sent, and issues of consent.

65. Avoid forensic evaluations of one's own patients.

66. When making formal assessments of the risk of violence, familiarize yourself with actuarial prediction instruments.

67. Select generally accepted assessment instruments that are readily available and reasonably relied on by experts in the relevant scientific community and that have reasonable reliability and validity data.

68. Use procedures that standardize administration, scoring, and interpretation of assessment instruments.

69. Assess a wide range of relevant variables with at least several tests per variable as a way to meet the criterion of comprehensiveness and to reduce the error rate.

70. Use empirically supported instruments to assess response style and other factors that might affect the validity of self-reports, such as malingering.

71. Evaluate other relevant sources of data in addition to psychological testing, such as medical records, deposition and trial testimony, and so forth.

72. Disclose the limits of the evidence and how such limits might affect the certainty of the expert opinions as well as disclosure of reasonable alternative explanations for the evidence.

patients. In rare cases—geographic unavailability of other clinicians or unique training or knowledge—you may be drafted into the expert role, though this may alter the treatment relationship" (#22, Gutheil, 2004). These differing positions reflect agreement that simultaneous professional roles of treating clinician and forensic evaluator should typically be avoided, but also describe the exceptions in a range from "none mentioned" to "whenever (it is not) possible" to "unavailability of other clinicians or unique training or knowledge."

Functional Legal Capacities

The importance of functional legal capacities is stressed in three of these practice guidelines. These include identifying the functional capacity that is directly relevant to the legal question (#29, Simon & Gold, 2004b), explaining the relationship between the diagnosis and the functional capacity (#30, Simon & Gold, 2004b), and not substituting a diagnosis for the careful evaluation of the functional capacity (#31, Simon & Gold, 2004b). This emphasis on the importance of the functional capacities is consistent with the broader forensic literature and may be seen in earlier descriptions of a "model" for the FMHA process (Grisso, 1986, 2003; Morse, 1978).

Data-Gathering, Interpretation, and Communication

There is also discussion of FMHA data-gathering, interpretation, and communication. It begins with the importance of the referral question: "Be clear on the forensic question being asked" (#63; Thompson, LeBourgeois, & Black, 2004). Guided by honesty and striving for objectivity (#20, Gutheil, 2004), which in turn is checked through self-monitoring of case selection (#33, Wettstein, 2004) and pattern of forensic opinions (#41, Wettstein, 2004), forensic psychiatrists are urged to take a number of steps when conducting an FMHA. They should *request missing data from the attorney* (#18, Gutheil, 2004), *render an opinion supportable by the data* (#19, Gutheil, 2004), *base diagnoses when possible on objective data* (#52, Gerbasi, 2004), *perform multiple interviews with the evaluee* (#36, Wettstein, 2004), *obtain corroborative data* (#37, Wettstein, 2004), *use all available data from collateral sources, interview, and testing to formulate well-reasoned opinions* (#57, Zonana, Roth, & Coric, 2004), and *fully substantiate and disclose limitations of opinions* (#41–#42, Wettstein, 2004). Specialized questions such as malingering and violence risk should be informed when necessary by conducting specialized testing (#61, Thompson, LeBourgeois, & Black, 2004; #66, Mossman, 2004).

Implications for Best Practice

The Simon and Gold volume was apparently not written with the goal of developing broad FMHA practice guidelines and is oriented primarily toward forensic psychiatrists. Nevertheless, considering the proffered guidelines across (rather than within) chapter topics and their consistency supports the notion that many do apply broadly. We now turn to a section that describes FMHA components across a wide range of legal questions, focusing on the foundational aspects of forensic assessment.

Principles: Melton and Colleagues

In their discussion of the nature and method of forensic assessment, Melton et al. (2007) focus on four broad domains. First, they describe the differences between forensic and *therapeutic* assessment. (The latter is a term also used by Heilbrun [2001] to connote mental health evaluation conducted for the purposes of diagnosis and treatment planning.) Second, they discuss psychological assessment techniques in three domains and how each applies to FMHA. Third, they address the role of archival and third party information, describing both why and how such data are used in forensic assessment. Finally, they note the importance of assessing response style, also discussing various ways in which self-report can be distorted and offering strategies for assessing each response style (see Table 4.2).

Therapeutic versus Forensic Assessment

The differences between therapeutic and forensic assessment are first itemized.

SCOPE

FMHA tends to focus on nonclinical events or interactions that are narrowly defined. Broader issues such as diagnosis or treatment planning, which are prominent in therapeutic evaluation, play a much less prominent role in FMHA.

IMPORTANCE OF CLIENT'S PERSPECTIVE

The "client" in therapeutic assessment is typically the individual who is being evaluated. It is that individual's perspective that is most important in the assessment, with "objective" appraisal secondary in importance.

Table 4.2	Nature and Method of Forensic Assessment (Material adapted from Melton et al., 2007.)

- Therapeutic and forensic assessment differ in

  - Scope
  - Importance of client's perspective
  - Voluntariness
  - Autonomy
  - Threats to validity
  - Relationship and dynamics
  - Pace and setting

- Psychological assessment techniques apply differently according to forensic specialization

  - *Clinical assessment instruments* (psychological tests and assessment approaches initially developed for use in assessment, diagnosis, and treatment planning in therapeutic contexts)
  - *Forensically relevant instruments* (assess clinical constructs that are most relevant to the evaluation of persons involved in the legal system)
  - *Forensic assessment instruments* (designed for use in the legal process; assess psycholegal capacities, abilities, or knowledge)

- Archival and third party information often inform the forensic evaluation

  - Forensic evaluations have a greater need for accuracy
  - There are differences in response style between persons in therapeutic and forensic evaluation contexts
  - Forensic evaluation conclusions receive greater scrutiny

- Response style should be formally assessed

  - Feigning of symptoms
  - Feigned thought disorder
  - Feigned intellectual impairment
  - Feigned anxiety and depression
  - Denial, guardedness, and minimization

By contrast, the "client" in FMHA is the referral source—the court, attorney, or agency that has requested the evaluation. The forensic clinician endeavors to provide this client with information that is not yet known. The value of "objective" appraisal is high, accordingly, with the perspective of the individual being evaluated secondary.

VOLUNTARINESS

Most individuals who seek mental health treatment do so voluntarily. By contrast, FMHA is conducted with individuals who are involved in litigation, at the request of an attorney, court, agency, or other party. Choices are much more limited in the context of FMHA, and often (e.g., as when the evaluation is ordered by the court) the individual has no legal right to refuse to participate.

AUTONOMY

Related to the issue of voluntariness, those undergoing therapeutic assessment enjoy greater autonomy and have more input into the process of the assessment, including objectives and procedures. The parameters of the legal context define the boundaries of FMHA.

THREATS TO VALIDITY

Melton and colleagues note that distortion of self-reported information is a threat to validity in both therapeutic and forensic assessments. However, those undergoing FMHA usually have something important to gain (or lose) from the legal decision. Therefore, they have greater motivation to *deliberately, intentionally* distort self-reported information.

RELATIONSHIP AND DYNAMICS

Therapeutic assessment is part of the larger process of mental health treatment. Caring, trust, and the intention to help are important aspects of this process. Those conducting FMHA should be open about their purpose and respectful in their interactions, but it would be ethically improper to convey the intent to be helpful in the same way that treating clinicians do. The "working alliance" of the therapist and client explicitly incorporates the idea that therapy is being conducted to be helpful in this way. By contrast, there is a certain emotional distance that results from the forensic clinician's (quite proper) attempt to remain impartial and convey results accurately, even if they are not necessarily helpful to the individual being evaluated.

PACE AND SETTING

In therapeutic assessment, one often has the luxury of being able to proceed with the pace of treatment—even adding to the assessment, correcting inaccuracies, as treatment is ongoing. FMHA, by contrast, is affected by the schedule of the litigation and the "finality" of the court's decision. The forensic clinician does not have the luxury of correcting an inaccurate or incomplete report after the legal decision has been made. Every effort must be made to be reasonably complete and accurate when the report is submitted.

Psychological Assessment Techniques

In their discussion of the second broad domain of FMHA, Melton et al. (2007) turn to psychological assessment techniques that may be useful. They note the distinction between clinical assessment instruments, forensically relevant instruments, and forensic assessment instruments (see Heilbrun, Rogers, & Otto, 2002, for a fuller discussion). *Clinical assessment instruments* are those developed for assessment, diagnosis, and treatment-planning in therapeutic contexts, but do not measure constructs that are typically of central importance in forensic assessment. By contrast, *forensically relevant instruments* were developed in the same way, but address constructs that are more central in criminal and civil litigation (such as response style) and may have undergone additional validation with these populations. *Forensic assessment instruments* (Grisso, 1986, 2003) are tools that have been developed specifically for use in litigation. They measure constructs that are central to specific legal questions and are used only in the context of that specific kind of litigation. Their validation is conducted with those in the population associated with this specific legal question.

It is useful to consider psychological assessment instruments in this way. As Melton et al. point out, the use of a forensic assessment instrument that has been specifically developed for and validated on the legal issue at focus in a given FMHA is highly desirable.

Forensically relevant instruments are less central but still important, particularly when they measure a construct that is an important part of a given assessment. By contrast, clinical assessment instruments are typically of little demonstrable relevance; their use may even be counterproductive, as using such "psychological tests" may convey the misimpression that important and relevant information is being provided. Traditional instruments may help explain why an evaluee is or is not legally competent. Such instruments may assist in providing an explanation to the judge or jury for the psycholegal opinion, contributing to the credibility of the findings. Like other sources of data in FMHA, however, psychological test results would never, by themselves, be sufficient to appropriately answer a psycholegal question.

Third Party Information

Melton et al.'s third point emphasizes the importance of third party information in FMHA. Both the need for greater accuracy and the reality of greater scrutiny in the adversarial system suggest that forensic clinicians are well advised to review and incorporate archival documents and interviews with collateral observers into FMHA. In addition, Melton et al. point out that the greater threat to validity resulting from the evaluee's incentive to deliberately distort information calls for a management strategy that includes multiple sources of information. Accordingly, they suggest that third party information be considered a very important aspect of the FMHA.

It is also important to be specific about possible distortions in self-reported information. The authors discuss the feigning of symptoms generally, as well as the more specific feigning of thought disorder, intellectual impairment, and anxiety/depression. They also address the important matter of self-report distortions in the opposite direction: denial, guardedness, and minimization. Forensic clinicians should always be aware of the possibility of distorted self-report, but should have specific strategies for appraising the extent of such distortion and its impact on self-reported information when there are preliminary indicators of responding in a deliberately inaccurate fashion during an FMHA.

Principles: Heilbrun and Colleagues

Heilbrun (2001) described a broader set of principles that are intended to apply to all types of FMHA. These principles incorporated the existing literatures in the areas of law, science, ethics, and practice. The description of their derivation and consistency with sources of authority from these areas was preceded by a discussion of the differences between forensic assessment and that conducted for diagnostic and treatment-planning purposes ("therapeutic assessment," as discussed also by Melton et al., 2007). These differences may be seen in Table 4.3. Subsequent work has addressed how these principles can be applied to a broad range of forensic assessment in civil (although not yet juvenile) and criminal areas (Heilbrun, Marczyk, & DeMatteo, 2002), and to more-specific areas such as capital sentencing (Heilbrun, DeMatteo, Marczyk, Finello, Smith, & Mack-Allen, 2005; Marczyk, Knauss, Kutinsky, DeMatteo, & Heilbrun, 2007), forensic neuropsychological assessment (Heilbrun, Marczyk, DeMatteo, Zillmer, Harris, & Jennings, 2003), sexual offender assessment (Heilbrun, 2003), and FMHA evaluation quality (Heilbrun, DeMatteo, & Marczyk, 2004). It should be noted that current efforts to identify FMHA principles have been wholly conceptual in nature. Determining whether such principles improve FMHA quality will require considerable empirical research.

This section will begin by summarizing the derivation and organization of these principles. Each principle will then be described briefly.

Purposes and Organization of Principles

Identifying broad, foundational principles of FMHA could serve three purposes, according to Heilbrun (2001). The first would be training. Providing principles applicable to various forms of FMHA would allow trainees to develop a solid background in forensic assessment and facilitate the acquisition of additional expertise in particular domains within FMHA. Second, such principles could promote theory and research linking the components of FMHA and allow such linkage across domains as well. Third, if foundational principles serve to make FMHA more uniform, consistent, and thorough, it should improve the quality of practice and also have implications for policy.

Table 4.3 Therapeutic Versus Forensic Assessment: Relevant Differences (Table from Heilbrun, 2001, p.9, reprinted with permission from Springer.)

	Therapeutic	**Forensic**
Purpose	Diagnose and treat symptoms of illness	Assist decision-maker or attorney
Examiner-Examinee Relationship	Helping role	Objective or quasi-objective stance
Notification of Purpose	Implicit assumptions about purpose shared by doctor and patient Formal, explicit notification typically not done	Assumptions about purpose not necessarily shared Formal and explicit notification
Who is Being Served	Individual patient	Variable; may be court, attorney, and client
Nature of Standard Being Considered	Medical, psychiatric, psychological	Medical, psychiatric, psychological, and legal
Data Sources	Self-report Psychological testing Behavioral assessment Medical procedures	Self-report Psychological testing Behavioral assessment Medical procedures Observations of others Relevant legal documents
Response Style of Examinee	Assumed to be reliable	Not assumed to be reliable
Clarification of Reasoning and Limits on Knowledge	Optional	Very important
Written Report	Brief, conclusory note	Lengthy and detailed Documents findings, reasoning, and conclusions
Court Testimony	Not expected	Expected

Table 4.4 Principles of Forensic Mental Health Assessment
(Material adapted from Heilbrun, 2001.)

1. Identify relevant forensic issues.
2. Accept referrals only within area of expertise.
3. Decline the referral when evaluator impartiality is unlikely.
4. Clarify the evaluator's role with the attorney.
5. Clarify financial arrangements.
6. Obtain appropriate authorization.
7. Avoid playing the dual roles of therapist and forensic evaluator.
8. Determine the particular role to be played within forensic assessment if the referral is accepted.
9. Select the most appropriate model to guide data gathering, interpretation, and communication.
10. Use multiple sources of information for each area being assessed.
11. Use relevance and reliability (validity) as guides for seeking information and selecting data sources.
12. Obtain relevant historical information.
13. Assess clinical characteristics in relevant, reliable, and valid ways.
14. Assess legally relevant behavior.
15. Ensure that conditions for evaluation are quiet, private, and distraction-free.
16. Provide appropriate notification of purpose and/or obtain appropriate authorization before beginning.
17. Determine whether the individual understands the purpose of the evaluation and the associated limits on confidentiality.
18. Use third party information in assessing response style.
19. Use testing when indicated in assessing response style.
20. Use case-specific (idiographic) evidence in assessing clinical condition, functional abilities, and causal connection.
21. Use nomothetic evidence is assessing clinical condition, functional abilities, and causal connection.

continued

22. Use scientific reasoning in assessing causal connection between clinical condition and functional abilities.

23. Do not answer the ultimate legal question.

24. Describe findings and limits so that they need change little under cross examination.

25. Attribute information to sources.

26. Use plain language; avoid technical jargon.

27. Write report in sections, according to model and procedures.

28. Base testimony on the results of the properly performed FMHA.

29. Testify effectively.

Table 4.4 identifies Heilbrun's (2001) 29 foundational principles of FMHA. These are ordered sequentially according to stages of FMHA: preparation, data collection, data interpretation, and communication. Each principle was discussed according to its support from relevant authorities in the areas of law, ethics, behavioral and medical science, and practice, as was discussed in more detail in Chapter 3. These sources of authority were considered for each principle. This allowed each of the principles to be categorized as *established* (largely supported by research, accepted in practice, and consistent with ethical and legal standards, as judged by the author) or *emerging* (supported in some areas, with mixed or absent evidence from others, or supported by some evidence, with continuing disagreement among professionals regarding their application, again according to the author's judgment).

Specific Principles

Each of these 29 FMHA principles is now summarized, along with an indication as to whether each is presently classified as established or emerging.

IDENTIFY RELEVANT FORENSIC ISSUES

There is an important distinction between the legal question, as the ultimate matter to be decided by the court, and the relevant forensic issues, which are capacities and abilities that are a part of the ultimate legal question. Making this distinction early serves several purposes. It identifies the proper focus for FMHA, both in practice and in research, as capacities (sometimes also called "functional legal capacities") that can be assessed and measured by forensic clinicians. It also helps explain the "ultimate issue" controversy that has been debated in the field of forensic assessment for over two decades (see, e.g., Grisso, 1986, 2003; Melton et al., 1987, 1997, 2007; Rogers & Ewing, 1989; Tillbrook, Mumley, & Grisso, 2003; and the discussion in Chapter 3 of this volume), as the forensic issues can be appraised and the results communicated in a way that does not require the evaluator to incorporate the moral and community values that are inevitably a part of the ultimate legal decision. This principle was classified as *established*.

ACCEPT REFERRALS ONLY WITHIN AREA OF EXPERTISE

The notion that professionals should be competent and knowledgeable about the services they deliver is so widely cited and apparently accepted that it is certainly not unique to forensic assessment. However, the question of what constitutes expertise in the area of FMHA is more specific. Education, training, and experience are recognized as important aspects of expertise, according to both ethical standards and evidence law. According to the American Bar Association's *Criminal Justice Mental Health Standards,* expertise for the purpose of FMHA would include:

1. sufficient professional education and sufficient clinical training and experience to establish the clinical knowledge required for the specific type(s) of evaluation(s) being conducted; and

2. sufficient forensic knowledge, gained through specialized training or an acceptable substitute thereof, necessary for understanding the relevant legal matter(s) and for satisfying the specific purpose(s) for which the evaluation is being ordered (Standard 7–3.10, 1989, p. 130).

These two components emphasize both foundational expertise gained through clinical and didactic training and specific experience with such populations, and specific experience through the application of this expertise in a forensic context. The principle was considered *established*.

DECLINE THE REFERRAL WHEN EVALUATOR IMPARTIALITY IS UNLIKELY

Impartiality does not mean that forensic clinicians are not human. Litigation involves individuals who have allegedly behaved in ways that can elicit a range of emotions from the forensic clinician, including shock, sadness, and anger. But the crucial test involves whether such reactions, or other circumstances of the evaluation, would keep the forensic clinician from conducting an evaluation that is thorough, fair, and accurate—or would keep the evaluator from moving from data to whatever conclusions are best supported by such data. An evaluator questioning her own impartiality prior to accepting a referral might use the following test. When there are two different conclusions that the evaluator could draw based on the FMHA (call them A and B), she might ask herself, "What would be my response if the outcome were A? What if the outcome were B?" When the answers to these questions differ sharply, whether for professional, financial, or emotional reasons, it is likely that she could not be impartial in that particular case and should decline the referral.

There are four possible roles for the mental health professional in litigation: court-appointed, expert for the defense, prosecution, or plaintiff, consultant, and fact witness. Being court-appointed involves an order from the judge accompanied by the expectation that the resulting FMHA will be considered without being introduced by either side. Experts for one side involved in the litigation may be appointed by the court in some jurisdictions, but with the expectation that the FMHA will be used as evidence at the discretion of the attorney for that litigant. It can also include referrals from attorneys in which the authorization comes directly from that attorney and not via the court. Consultants, by contrast, are requested by one of the litigants to help in a variety of ways (e.g., prepare the attorney to challenge an expert for opposing counsel, review the professional or scientific literatures to provide support for a given legal argument) but do not conduct their own evaluation or testify as experts. Finally, "fact witness" is a role that a treating clinician could adopt if he is unsuccessful in avoiding any role whatsoever it litigation involving his patient. This role does not involve rendering opinions, but (like any fact witness) testifying only to what he has directly observed. Serving as a fact witness does not mean, necessarily, that a mental health professional lacks forensic expertise—only that he did not assume the role of a forensic expert from the beginning, and hence gather information in a way that would allow him to testify as a forensic expert.

This principle urging that one should decline referrals when one cannot be impartial was considered *established* when the forensic clinician is either court appointed or an expert for the defense, prosecution, or plaintiff, but it was considered *neither established nor emerging* when the forensic clinician assumes the role of consultant. That is, impartiality is important for every identifiable role a forensic clinician might play, except for that of consultant. Providing information in a way that is not impartial to an attorney who has hired the forensic clinician to provide consultation for the purpose of winning the case does not appear harmful or unethical.

CLARIFY THE EVALUATOR'S ROLE WITH THE ATTORNEY

Playing multiple roles in a single case often creates conflicts that threaten the integrity of one's work. The roles described in the discussion of the previous principle should, almost without exception, be mutually exclusive. Just as it is unethical to combine a forensic evaluation with a treatment role ("dual roles" as described by the *Ethics Code;* "dual agency" as noted by several authors in Simon & Gold, 2003), it is likewise problematic to play more than one forensic role in the same case. This principle describes the importance of identifying which of these roles the evaluator will play, and confirming in an early discussion with the attorney that it will be the single role played throughout. There is one possible exception, which is discussed later in Principle #8 ("Determine the particular role to be played within forensic assessment if the referral is accepted"). This principle was considered *emerging* at the time it was discussed. In light of the increasing focus on avoiding dual role conflicts seen in psychology and psychiatry during the last decade, it might be consider *established* today.

CLARIFY FINANCIAL ARRANGEMENTS

FMHA services often are provided in the course of one's salaried employment. In contrast, when FMHA services are billed, arrangements are somewhat different from billing for clinical services. They may be billed at a higher rate, particularly when provided by forensic specialists.

They are typically billed to a court, an attorney, or a larger jurisdiction (e.g., a city, the federal government), but not to insurance companies and not directly to the individual being evaluated. Applicable procedures are likely to be familiar to referring attorneys. However, some attorneys may ask the forensic clinician to collect a fee directly from the individual being evaluated, which can contribute to the misperception that this individual (rather than the attorney or the court) is the primary client in FMHA. Questions about hourly rate or total fee should be answered in advance of beginning the evaluation, however, and the forensic clinician should never put herself in the position of having the collection of an evaluation fee be contingent on the outcome of the evaluation. It is only when the financial questions are answered by existing law or policy (for example, a jurisdiction may set the overall fee for a particular kind of evaluation, and deviate from that amount only under rare circumstances and upon expressed justification) that this principle need not apply. This principle was considered *established*.

OBTAIN APPROPRIATE AUTHORIZATION

Different kinds of authorization are needed, depending on the role played by the forensic clinician in a particular case. When court-appointed, the forensic clinician needs authorization (typically in the form of a court order) from the judge. When acting as an expert for the defense, prosecution, or plaintiff, the forensic clinician should have the authorization of both the referring attorney (which is implicit but sufficient when the attorney requests the evaluation from the forensic clinician) and the individual being evaluated. This synchronicity between role and nature of authorization has further implications for the nature of the request to the individual being evaluated, which will be discussed later in this section in the context of the principles of delivering notification of purpose or obtaining informed consent, and determining whether the individual understood the notification. This principle was considered *established*.

AVOID PLAYING THE DUAL ROLES OF THERAPIST AND FORENSIC EVALUATOR

This principle describes a particular kind of "dual role" or "dual agency." When a clinician is involved in the delivery of treatment services to an individual, and subsequently provides a forensic evaluation and possible testimony with that same individual, he is playing two distinct professional roles with the same individual. The conflicts that this creates are clear when one considers the differences between therapeutic and forensic assessment (see Table 4.3). The nature of the relationship between clinician and patient differs between these two roles: it is very difficult to become objective when one has previously been a treating therapist advocating the patient's best interest. Since the primary goals of each role differ substantially, it would be very unlikely that the original treatment agreement would encompass subsequent forensic assessment and its noteworthy differences. The clinician proceeds using some different sources of information and an approach to assessment that emphasizes the patient's perspective primarily, versus a comprehensive picture painted by multiple sources of information. Finally, the written report and the possibility of court testimony both differ substantially. The activities are sufficiently different that it is virtually impossible for a single mental health professional to do both well with the same individual. In addition, the change in the relationship that would result from the forensic assessment would be likely to adversely affect the treatment interactions. This principle was considered *established*.

DETERMINE THE PARTICULAR ROLE TO BE PLAYED WITHIN FORENSIC ASSESSMENT IF THE REFERRAL IS ACCEPTED

This principle specifies playing a single role throughout the entire FMHA case. The role should be selected and agreed upon in the beginning. It does encompass extra-FMHA professional dual roles like therapist–forensic evaluator (see discussion of previous principle), but mainly focuses on the different roles *within* FMHA described in the earlier principle of declining a referral when impartiality is not possible. Staying within a single FMHA role can help ensure that the expectations of the attorney and the forensic clinician are consistent.

There is one potential exception to this general dictum. It involves moving from a role requiring impartiality (e.g., defense expert expected to testify) to a role in which impartiality is not needed (e.g., consultant) when it is apparent that the attorney will not request a report or testimony because of the nature of the FMHA results. However, moving in the opposite direction (from consultant, which does not require impartiality, to testifying expert, which does) would be far more difficult and is not recommended. This principle was classified as *emerging*.

SELECT THE MOST APPROPRIATE MODEL TO GUIDE DATA GATHERING, INTERPRETATION, AND COMMUNICATION

This principle addresses the value in using an appropriate FMHA model during data gathering, interpretation, and communication. Two models in particular have been described. The first (Morse, 1978) is the simpler of the two. There are three broad questions addressed by many different kinds of mental health law, which constitute the structure of this model:

- The existence of a mental disorder
- The functional abilities related to the tasks that are part of the relevant legal question, and
- The causal connection between mental disorder and functional abilities (or deficits).

Grisso (1986) described a somewhat more complex FMHA model with six components:

1. *Functional* abilities—what an individual can do or accomplish, as well as specific knowledge, understanding, or beliefs related to the legal question.

2. *Contextual*—the general environment establishing parameters for defining the relevance of particular functional abilities for the legal question.

3. *Causal* inferences—describing the relationship between an individual's functional abilities or deficits and the legal question.

4. *Interactive* characteristic—does this person's relevant functional abilities meet the demands of the situation with which the individual was or will be faced?

5. *Judgment*—whether the person–context incongruency is sufficient to warrant a legal finding of incompetence and its disposition.

6. *Disposition*—consequences of the legal finding, which may give the state the authority to act in some way toward the individual.

In Grisso's more recent (2003) description of this model, the six components were reduced to five, combining the functional and contextual components into a broader functional domain.

This principle was considered *emerging* when discussed in 2001. It would probably be classified as *established* today. As Grisso (2003) observed, it has guided research and practice since it first appeared, and has not been seriously challenged for accuracy or relevance. Moreover, there is considerable overlap between the Morse and Grisso models. Both specify functional and causal components, crucial elements of FMHA, as evaluators seek to describe the causal relationship between certain clinical/personality variables and functional-legal capacities. It should be added that these two models apply reasonably well to FMHA in the areas of civil commitment, criminal competencies, and mental state at the time of the offense. They apply less well to child custody evaluations, in which clinical variables typically do not play a prominent role and complexity is greatly increased by having two parents' capacities considered in the context of the child's (sometimes the children's) best interests. They also would apply poorly to personal injury evaluations, in which the evaluator is guided by the elements of tort law. It would certainly be possible to construct a model that applies to child custody evaluations and another that applies to personal injury evaluations. It simply has not yet been done—and we do not encourage forensic clinicians to use a model that does not fit the particular evaluation they are conducting.

USE MULTIPLE SOURCES OF INFORMATION FOR EACH AREA BEING ASSESSED

There are two main reasons that FMHA places a heavy emphasis on obtaining information about individuals' capacities or characteristics from multiple sources. First, individuals evaluated in legal contexts often have some incentive to distort the accuracy of their self-report. This is discussed in detail by Melton et al. (2007; see Table 4.2), who also comment about the potential usefulness of third party information in managing this difficulty. Second, even without intending to be deceptive, any single informant may simply offer an inaccurate or biased perspective. The same may be said for any single psychological measure. Agreement across multiple sources of information, such as self-report, collateral records, and psychological testing, specialized forensic testing, and collateral interviews, makes it more likely that the information is accurate (Heilbrun, Warren, & Picarello, 2003; Kraemer, Kazdin, Offord, Kessler, Jensen, & Kupfer, 1997; Otto, Slobogin, & Greenberg, 2007). The antecedents of this approach appear in the multitrait-multimethod matrix (Campbell & Fiske, 1959), which is a powerful validity measurement approach on both quantitative and commonsense levels. This principle was considered *established*.

USE RELEVANCE AND RELIABILITY (VALIDITY) AS GUIDES FOR SEEKING INFORMATION AND SELECTING DATA SOURCES

Relevance and reliability are frequently cited in evidentiary law regarding the admissibility of expert testimony. Expert evidence must be relevant to the question(s) before the court and reliable (including both psychometric reliability and validity when used in the law). This principle underscores the importance of using both relevance and reliability as guides when deciding which sources of information to use, particularly when selecting which third parties to interview and which psychological tests to administer. Standard psychological tests and specialized forensic assessment instruments should have their psychometric properties described in a manual before they are selected for use in FMHA (see Heilbrun, Rogers, & Otto, 2002), so appraising their published psychometric properties, established through peer-reviewed research, should be straightforward. Estimating the validity of interviewing procedures, particularly third party interviews, is far more difficult. A helpful description of the strategy for selecting an interviewee has been provided (Kraemer et al., 1997); it involves first selecting the individual who knows the evaluee best, but selecting the next third party from among those who know the evaluee best from a different context. For example, if the first person interviewed were a family member, the second individual selected would be from a different domain (e.g., school, job, or church). This principle was considered *established*.

OBTAIN RELEVANT HISTORICAL INFORMATION

This principle stresses the consistent importance of considering historical information about the individual being evaluated in FMHA. There are various kinds of FMHA in which a more extensive history is needed (e.g., capital sentencing), and other types in which the history can be more focused (e.g., competence to stand trial). But the history required for any kind of FMHA is usually greater than that for diagnostic and treatment-planning purposes. Among other important contributions, a history constructed from multiple sources can help the forensic clinician gauge the accuracy of the evaluee's self-report, which can be particularly important for considering response style (discussed in subsequent principles). This principle was considered *established*.

ASSESS CLINICAL CHARACTERISTICS IN RELEVANT, RELIABLE, AND VALID WAYS

The matters of which clinical characteristics to assess and how to assess them, are questions that can be guided by the evidentiary criteria of relevance and reliability. For the purposes of this principle, *clinical characteristics* is defined broadly. There are some forms of FMHA in which it is unlikely that mental health is the exclusive, or even primary, consideration for this domain. Child custody is one example. Assessing divorcing spouses to gauge fitness for parenting is affected by a broader range of personality variables and life skills (which in turn affect functional capacities of parenting skills and motivation) than would result from a focus primarily on clinical symptoms. Juvenile transfer is a second example. The forensic clinician conducting this kind of FMHA must focus on a range of domains that include family, peers, educational, leisure time skills, and motivational as well as mental health issues. Assessing "clinical characteristics" selectively (according to relevance to the legal question) and accurately (reliably and validly) depends on taking a thoughtful approach in selecting psychological tests and specialized forensic assessment instruments validated for this particular purpose and with this population. This principle was considered *established*.

ASSESS LEGALLY RELEVANT BEHAVIOR

This principle addresses the capacities and behavior that are related to the specific legal question addressed in an FMHA. In many respects, this principle is at the heart of FMHA. Each of the other authors cited in this chapter who discuss guidelines for or components of FMHA (Melton et al., 2007; Simon & Gold, 2003) clearly describes the importance of functional legal capacities. Both of the models discussed under Principle #9 (Grisso, 1986, 2003; Morse, 1978) include a functional legal component that refers to *legally relevant* behavior. For some forms of FMHA, the forensic clinician now has the option of using a well-validated forensic assessment instrument (see Grisso, 2003). The principle was considered to be *established*.

ENSURE THAT CONDITIONS FOR EVALUATION ARE QUIET, PRIVATE, AND DISTRACTION-FREE

FMHA is often performed in settings that are not designed for mental health evaluations. "Secure institutions" such as jails, prisons, inpatient forensic units, and juvenile detention facilities may be noisy, allow sensitive material to be overheard, or present other distractions. This principle considers a balance between reasonable evaluation conditions and other considerations (e.g., security, time, and available space constraints). It addresses the question of when a forensic clinician should seek to improve evaluation conditions that are unacceptably poor on three dimensions: quiet (limited noise), private (conversation cannot be overheard by staff or other residents of the facility), and distraction-free (auditory, visual, and ambient temperature). This principle was classified as *established*.

PROVIDE APPROPRIATE NOTIFICATION OF PURPOSE AND/OR OBTAIN APPROPRIATE AUTHORIZATION BEFORE BEGINNING

The forensic clinician can begin the evaluation in one of two ways, depending on how it has been authorized. If the court has ordered the evaluation, then the individual being assessed does not have a legal right to refuse participation. If the referral has come from the litigant's attorney, then that individual retains the right to decline to undergo FMHA. So it is *notification of purpose* or *informed consent*, respectively, that apply to each of these forms of authorization. The information provided by each is comparable: (a) the nature and purpose of the evaluation, (b) who authorized the evaluation, and (c) the associated limits on confidentiality, including how the individual's information might be used. In a court-ordered evaluation, the individual's participation in the evaluation is legally compelled, so it would not be appropriate for the forensic clinician to seek informed consent. However, providing "notification of purpose" is necessary—the individual should receive an explanation of the purpose of the evaluation and how the information will be used. Providing such an explanation may serve to promote informed participation, an important part of the relationship that will facilitate gathering relevant and accurate information. When an attorney retains a forensic clinician to perform a forensic assessment of the attorney's client, however, the evaluation is voluntary; informed consent is therefore necessary in order for the evaluation to proceed. This principle was considered *established*.

DETERMINE WHETHER THE INDIVIDUAL UNDERSTANDS THE PURPOSE OF THE EVALUATION AND ASSOCIATED LIMITS ON CONFIDENTIALITY

The individual being evaluated must understand the information provided in the informed consent or notification of purpose described in the previous principle, if this step is to be meaningful. This principle describes how the forensic clinician can appraise understanding by asking the evaluee to paraphrase and explain it. If it is not well understood, but the evaluee is willing to proceed, then that does not necessarily mean the evaluation cannot continue. It may be that the same deficits that interfere with his meaningful understanding of the notification information (in a court-ordered evaluation) would also keep the him from possessing adequate functional legal capacities, so stopping the evaluation at this point could create a Catch-22 that would not allow an evaluation to be conducted. If an evaluee's comprehension of the nature of the assessment and its use remains poor despite attempts by the expert to clarify this information by using simpler language, the expert may consider consulting the individual's attorney before proceeding with the FMHA. However, when an individual declines to participate in an evaluation that is requested by his attorney, the evaluator's response should be to ask why and to discuss this with the attorney. The principle was classified as *established*.

USE THIRD PARTY INFORMATION IN ASSESSING RESPONSE STYLE

One important component of FMHA is the systematic assessment of the response style of the individual being evaluated, especially if she is deliberately overreporting or underreporting relevant deficits or symptoms. This principle is quite consistent with points made by others in this chapter (Simon & Gold, 2003, see Table 4.1; Melton et al., 2007, see Table 4.2). This particular principle emphasizes the importance of (a) using collateral documents and third party informants in establishing a multi-source history, and (b) determining whether self-reported information is consistent with other sources and therefore more likely to be accurate. This principle was considered *established*.

USE TESTING WHEN INDICATED IN ASSESSING RESPONSE STYLE

This principle underscores the value of using psychological tests and specialized measures (e.g., measures specifically developed to assess malingering or defensiveness of mental disorder or cognitive impairment) in assessing an individual's response style. There were relatively few well-validated psychological tests or specialized measures that were available for this purpose in 2001, so this principle was considered *emerging* at that time. However, there has been substantial progress in developing and validating these specialized measures during the last seven years. Such a principle would probably be closer to being *established* at present (see Melton et al., 2007).

USE CASE-SPECIFIC (IDIOGRAPHIC) EVIDENCE IN ASSESSING CLINICAL CONDITION, FUNCTIONAL ABILITIES, AND CAUSAL CONNECTION

There are three ways science can be applied in FMHA. This principle describes the first. It is particular to the law, rather than to behavioral or medical science, but one of the most valuable ways FMHA can be conducted is to integrate *idiographic* evidence with *nomothetic* data (described in the next principle). Idiographic evidence, as described in Chapter 3, is specific to the circumstances of the case. It describes the individual's functioning and then compares it to his capacities and functioning at other times. Particularly consistent with the legal goal of individualized justice, this principle was considered *established*.

USE NOMOTHETIC EVIDENCE IN ASSESSING CLINICAL CONDITION, FUNCTIONAL ABILITIES, AND CAUSAL CONNECTION

The second way in which science can be applied to FMHA is through using scientific data obtained with multiple participants. Such group-based data is applied to a population similar to that from which individual being evaluated is drawn. Conventionally, it is used with psychological tests and forensic assessment instruments that have been developed and validated on similar populations. These measures assist the evaluator and the legal decision maker in understanding how the measured capacities of the individual being evaluated compare to others in "known groups," using the norms developed from such groups. This principle is particularly important when one is using empirical evidence to make informed legal decisions. It was considered *established*.

USE SCIENTIFIC REASONING IN ASSESSING CAUSAL CONNECTION BETWEEN CLINICAL CONDITION AND FUNCTIONAL ABILITIES

In some respects, the process of FMHA can be considered comparable to that of science. This principle draws upon that analogy. When the results obtained from one source of information (e.g., interview or psychological testing) are treated as "hypotheses to be verified" (Heilbrun, 1992) through further information obtained from additional sources of information, it may be particularly helpful. When such hypotheses are accepted or rejected according to how well they account for the greatest amount of information with the simplest explanation, the scientific principle of parsimony is applied. This principle was classified as *established*. It will be useful to consider the term *functional* somewhat flexibly in this series. There are certain kinds of forensic evaluations (e.g., continued hospitalization evaluation incorporating risk assessment) in which the "functional capacities" involve the ability to refrain from violent or other criminal/antisocial behavior.

DO NOT ANSWER THE ULTIMATE LEGAL QUESTION DIRECTLY

The question of whether forensic evaluators should answer the ultimate legal question has been debated in the forensic assessment literature for several decades, and was discussed in detail in Chapter 3. Some in this field (e.g., Rogers & Ewing, 1989; Rogers & Shuman, 2000) note that many judges and attorneys expect the forensic clinician to offer an ultimate legal opinion, and that doing so does not create problems. Others (e.g., Grisso, 1986, 2003; Tillbrook et al., 2003) stress the importance of focusing on forensic capacities but also observe that the ultimate legal question, which includes moral, political, and community values, is therefore not an appropriate focus for an FMHA. This debate has not been resolved, so this principle was considered *emerging*. As we noted in Chapter 3, however, it is appropriate to limit FMHA conclusions to forensic capacities whenever it is practical to do so.

DESCRIBE FINDINGS AND LIMITS SO THAT THEY NEED CHANGE LITTLE UNDER CROSS EXAMINATION

If FMHA findings are obtained through a careful and thorough process, using multiple sources of information, and with appropriate limitations explicitly acknowledged, then it is not likely that even an intense cross-examination will result in substantial changes in the forensic clinician's opinion. The evaluator has considered various alternative explanations for these findings—as noted in the principle on scientific reasoning just discussed. In effect, the forensic clinician has put her results through a series of self-imposed challenges before drawing conclusions. This is one of the purposes of a good cross-examination. Having already gone through this process, the forensic clinician is less likely to be affected by it (in terms of reconsidering her conclusions or acknowledging their weaknesses) than she would have been without this self-imposed cross-examination. This principle was considered *established*.

ATTRIBUTE INFORMATION TO SOURCES

The *Specialty Guidelines for Forensic Psychologists* (Committee on Ethical Guidelines for Forensic Psychologists, 1991) indicate that the value of careful documentation and the anticipation of the challenging of findings are particularly important in FMHA. This principle, regarding attribution of information to specific source(s), underscores the importance of both documentation and anticipation of challenge. Attributing information allows the opposing attorney or the judge to identify what information has been obtained from which sources. In addition, attributing information adds to the credibility of the evaluator's judgment about the meaning of information carefully documented from multiple sources. When an evaluator testifies in cases in which the FMHA was conducted some time in the past, it may be very difficult to rely on his memory to accurately identify the different kinds of data and the various results they yielded. Identifying and attributing by sources can make his testimony far more accurate, meaningful, and credible. This principle was considered *established*.

USE PLAIN LANGUAGE; AVOID TECHNICAL JARGON

Technical terms are generally unnecessary to convey the results of FMHA. Most of those who use FMHA reports or testimony are without specialized training in mental health, whether they are trained in the law (e.g., judges, attorneys) or typically without training in either mental health or the law (e.g., jurors). Therefore, it is important to avoid using technical terminology, or to define technical terms if their use cannot be avoided. The avoidance of technical language does not mean that findings are simplified or that complex information is distorted. Rather, efforts should be made to convey findings and the data they are based on in language that consumers of the report and testimony can understand. This principle was considered to be *established*.

WRITE REPORT IN SECTIONS, ACCORDING TO MODEL AND PROCEDURES

This principle suggests that writing an FMHA report should be guided by the previously described principles. A variety of report styles can be used (see, e.g., Heilbrun et al., 2002). Suggestions for sections in a report that are most consistent with these principles are as follows:

- *Referral* (information concerning the individual being evaluated, his characteristics, the nature of the evaluation and the associated legal question(s) and forensic capacities, and the referral source),

- *Procedures* (evaluation times and dates, tests or procedures used, records reviewed, and third party interviews conducted; documentation of the notification of purpose or informed consent and the degree to which the information appeared to be understood),

- *Relevant History* (containing information from multiple sources describing areas important to the evaluation, with breadth varying according to the nature of the evaluation),

- *Current Clinical Condition* (broadly considered to include appearance, mood, behavior, sensorium, intellectual functioning, thought, and personality, as well as information from other areas that may be relevant to the evaluation),

- *Forensic Capacities* (specifically according to the nature of the legal questions), and

- *Conclusions and Recommendations* (addressing the forensic capacities rather than the ultimate legal questions).

Some variations on this organization might also be consistent with these principles. For instance, some forensic clinicians might prefer to have separate sections for procedures and notification. Others might add a section entitled "Analysis" that draws upon the historical, clinical, and functional legal data to link them, through explicit reasoning, to the conclusions that are cited in the next section. This principle was considered *established*.

BASE TESTIMONY ON THE RESULTS OF THE PROPERLY PERFORMED FMHA

The substantive basis for an expert's conclusions and opinions that serve as the foundation for testimony should be documented in the FMHA report. This allows the presenting attorney to use the expert's findings more clearly and effectively, opposing counsel to prepare to challenge them and hence construct a more meaningful cross-examination, the judge to understand them, and the expert to communicate them. This principle was considered *established*.

TESTIFY EFFECTIVELY

This principle addresses two components of expert testimony: substance and style. The substantive part of expert testimony is composed of the FMHA guidelines, components, and principles discussed in this chapter. The "style" of expert testimony involves how the expert presents, dresses, speaks, and otherwise behaves, which can make testimony more understandable and credible. Strong substance *and* style in expert testimony is "best practice." Testimony that is substantively weak but stylistically impressive should not be considered a meaningful contribution to better-informed legal decision making, an important goal of FMHA. This principle was considered *established* if both substance and style are strong, but it was considered *neither established nor emerging* if the testimony is based on stylistic strength only.

Expert Testimony Maxims: Brodsky

In a series of books on expert testimony in FMHA, Brodsky (1991, 1999, 2004) has described a number of aspirational "maxims" that capture the essence of best practice in expert testimony extremely well. These maxims are listed in Table 4.5.

Table 4.5	Expert Testimony Maxims (Maxims from Brodsky, 1991, 1999, 2004, reprinted with permission.)

The following maxims are divided into **substantive** (related to the content and procedures of the forensic evaluation and its underlying empirical bases) and **procedural** (issues specific to expert mental health testimony and relevant to the effectiveness of the testimony).

SUBSTANTIVE MAXIMS

1. Respond to implications of being a bought expert by showing awareness of the issue and assertively presenting the foundations of your objectivity (1991).

2. Check and recheck that routine pulls toward affiliation are not diminishing the impartiality of the expert role (1991).

3. Review current literature on the topic about which you will testify (1991).

4. Burdens of proof and degrees of defined certainty are legal concepts. Do not accept, define, or incorporate them into clinical, psychological, or scientific testimony (1991).

5. Be prepared to present the bases for generalizability of findings and demographic communalities in your testimony (1991).

continued

6. Challenges to professional experience should be met with a knowledge of the literature and affirmations of the worth of your own experience (1991).

7. Do not change a professional opinion on the basis of a cross-examination. Your opinions should always arise from your data (1991).

8. Questions about children's lying and fantasies should be answered with open acknowledgment of their existence and the ways in which the clinical examination ruled them out as causes of the allegations of abuse (1991).

9. In the controversial area of anatomically detailed dolls in the assessment of child sexual abuse, witnesses should know both the criticisms and supporting data, as well as the requisite professional competencies that accompany their use (1991).

10. Challenges about clients faking bad or faking good should be met with affirmative statements of clinical validity, sensitivity, and vigilance for client dissimulation (1991).

11. Research on client dissimulation should be known and used in clinical work and testimony. Enough of the research findings are equivocal that caution in evaluations and witness statements are always in order (1991).

12. Good definitions are necessary but not sufficient bases for answering fundamental questions. Broader conceptual understanding is needed (1991).

13. Prepare a list of professionally relevant and complete qualifying questions for the attorney to use in the opening of the direct examination (1991).

14. Culture does affect the assessment of psychopathology. Witnesses should be culture educated while still clearly identifying and affirming the conventional foundations of their testimony (1991).

15. Do not be befuddled if you do not know specific DSM cautions. Do affirm the underlying principles of such cautions in which you believe (1991).

continued

16. In equal opportunity cases, plaintiff witnesses need to focus on social context and defense witnesses on objective comparisons (1991).

17. Cross-examinations about examiner effects call for the witness to explain how training and standardized procedures diminish such effects (1991).

18. From the earliest stage of legal activity, be certain to have mastered the foundations of your knowledge and role (1991).

19. Agree to be an expert only when genuine expertise is present (1991).

20. It is normal for psychotherapists to be reluctant or ambivalent when testifying about their clients. Testimony should include the strengths of the participant-observer role and the extended opportunities to observe their clients (1991).

21. When you truly do not know, say so (1991).

22. The heated emotionality of termination of parental rights hearings calls for exceptionally well-prepared and constructive testimony (1991).

23. With indifferent attorneys be assertive. With incompetent attorneys, decline the case or educate them (1991).

24. The Ziskin and Faust reviews have an adversarial component and consequently may not meet the respected minority test. Nevertheless, they have made us more accountable and that can be acknowledged constructively (1991).

25. The techniques here are not an impenetrable shield for unprepared witnesses. Weaknesses in methodology can and should be exposed by competent probing in the adversarial process (1999).

26. Keep the context of your assessments and findings as a foreground issue in expert testimony (1999).

27. Under *Daubert*, professional and scientific experts should be prepared with peer-reviewed research to defend the nature of their theories, principles, and methodologies (1999).

28. Never accept attorney condensation, summary, or conclusions as your only working materials. The expert's responsibility is to review and assess the case personally and professionally (1999).

continued

29. Keep your ethical priorities in order. Attending to scientific and professional truths always comes before responsibility to the court, and those court obligations always precede responsibilities to retaining counsel and to protecting one's self-esteem (1999).

30. Do not defend experience itself as proof of being accurate in forensic conclusions. Instead, report your career experience if asked, and address the specific skills and means of reaching your conclusions (1999).

31. Over-prepare: As in marriage, personal complacency can keep you from coping effectively with courtroom strife (1999).

32. Challenges to one's impartiality may be addressed by having calculated (for intrinsic reasons) the percentage of times one's expert opinions are contrary to those of retaining attorneys (1999).

33. Real ambiguities exist in understanding and interpreting behaviors of defendants and litigants. Opposing experts who disagree with you are not necessarily corrupt, dim, or myopic (1999).

34. Assumptions about what and how you are communicating on the stand need to be checked and rechecked (1999).

35. Evaluating experts can legitimately give up their roles as expert witnesses to become jury or trial consultants, but should never assume both roles, or shift from jury or trial consultants to becoming testifying experts (1999).

36. Silence becomes us when we are not intimidated by it in cross-examination and can use it comfortably toward our own effective testimony (1999).

37. Psychological disorders and labels are socially constructed, and the prepared expert knows the nature and limits of the constructs (1999).

38. Evaluations that are tape-recorded may be useful for maintaining an accurate and accountable record of questions and statements of both examiners and subjects (1999).

39. Do not be immediately agreeable to affirmations of common sense until you have thought through the specific meanings of the questions for your data, conclusions, and opinions (1999).

continued

40. Ultimate issue testimony should be approached with caution and considered a rare event that is dependent on the situation (1999).

41. Tell the story of what you have found and believe in a way that makes the technical material accessible and that enhances the jury's understanding of your opinion. Build a narrative bridge between your findings and the actual experience of the defendant or litigant so that the testimony comes alive to create a meaningful story (2004).

42. Treat the understanding of narrative technique in testimony as a serious and substantial undertaking with personal discipline, increased awareness, and systematic practice. Then tell your story (2004).

43. Metaphors can clarify and simplify technical parts of testimony. Challenges to metaphors are best met by defining limits of the metaphor and by placing it in an illustrative context (2004).

44. Credibility of testimony occasionally can revolve around brief questions and answers. Treat all of your testimony, even short and apparently insignificant answers, as important enough to think through and answer with care (2004).

45. When ingratiating attorneys try to lead you to bragging and to statements of self-inflated attainments, stay with the facts of your credentials and dispel the flattery ploy with self-contained and unimposing assurance (2004).

46. Deposition transcripts may be corrected only if the court reported was inaccurate, and not if the witness was inaccurate. Corrections in substance need to be discussed with counsel or await opportunities to elaborate during trial testimony (2004).

47. The credibility of expert opinion hinges on the accuracy of the evaluations on which that opinion is based. Inaccurate translations may cloud the accuracy of those evaluations. Take the responsibility to go beyond taking translations at face value (2004).

48. Headline testimony is risky business. If options are available, turn down all such invitations to be involved unless you are clearly suited for the task. Approach publicity and the media with caution and discretion, even if the evaluee has given permission. Master saying "no comment" (2004).

continued

49. Experts should not be surprised by negative perceptions by other professionals that they are biased. Such possible accusations are all the more reason to perform at high levels of knowledge and accountability (2004).

50. Evaluators and not attorneys need to define their customary standards of professional practice. Stay committed to what you do and how you do it, even in the face of attorney pressures (2004).

51. Establish the boundaries of testimony and expertise, and structure accordingly how and about what you will testify (2004).

52. Freely offer advice about substantive content of your testimony to attorneys who have retained you. As a witness, be cautious about being drawn into inappropriate advice giving (2004).

53. When cross-examination demands move to you personally, seek to decline the gambit and stay with the objective and specific purposes of your findings (2004).

54. When the cross-examining attorney seeks extrapolation of your findings and conclusions to specific situations, be careful not to go beyond the limits of what you have actually found and know (2004).

55. Read and know the essential scholarly resources in your field, listen to talks by those scholars, e-mail them with questions, and be prepared to rebut cross-examinations on those topics in personal–professional ways (2004).

56. Local expert witnesses of moderate credentials often are equal in persuasion or in complex cases may have an advantage over the big-name expert. They should focus on what they know and have found, and try not to compare themselves to impressively credentialed persons who also testify (2004).

57. Even poised and knowledgeable professionals can be muddled and ineffective on the stand. During cross-examinations, think through the actual connections between your findings and the questions asked during cross. Answer in terms that are meaningful for your conclusions (2004).

58. Data errors can creep into testimony in many forms. One cannot be too compulsive in checking one's basic data (2004).

continued

59. Good testimony starts with good methods. Expert witnesses should be prepared to discuss criticisms in the literature of their methods in a manner that is knowledgeable, candid, and contextual.

60. Be prepared for challenges to basic concepts and accuracy by mobilizing relevant data and by acknowledging the context and limitations of your conclusions (2004).

61. Testify about psychological, not legislative or legal constructs, and integrate research and knowledge into carefully delineated predictions (2004).

62. Testimony about actuarial applications calls for being comfortably seated in the context, strengths, and weaknesses of such data (2004).

PROCEDURAL MAXIMS

1. Handle loaded and half-truth questions by first admitting the true part in a dependent clause and then strongly denying the untrue part in an independent clause (1991).

2. When challenged about insufficient experience, keep track of the true sources of your expertise (1991).

3. Criticize your field as requested, but be poised and matter of fact and look for opportunities to regain control (1991).

4. Witnesses often feel like aliens in the courtroom: The solution is to be present often and to develop a sense of place identify (1991).

5. Comfortably agree with accurate challenges to your credentials. Offer narrative explanations only when they are non-defensive and unforced (1991).

6. Meet with the attorney prior to the direct examination and be involved in preparing the questions (1991).

7. After a disaster during testimony, correct the error as soon as you can. If you cannot, let it go (1991).

8. Testimony about elder abuse calls for a mixture of specific expertise and visible empathy (1991).

9. When the attorney fishes for ignorance and insecurities, keep your knowledge limits clearly in mind (1991).

continued

10. Neither fraternize nor discuss any element of the case with opposing counsel, other witnesses, clients, or jurors (1991).

11. When testifying about something in which you believe, testify in a manner that shows that you believe in it (1991).

12. The historic hysteric gambit is an indication that nothing else has worked for the attorney. Respond with poise, either declining to discuss the historical events or dismissing them as obsolete and not applicable (1991).

13. If you are humorous at all on the witness stand, keep it gentle, good-natured, and infrequent (1991).

14. When attorneys try to intimidate, respond with controlling answers, proper manners, and clinical reflections (1991).

15. Explicitly relax or engage in productive work just before your court appearance (1991).

16. Effective language usage comes about when the witness personalizes answers, varies the format, uses narrative well, and produces convincing spoken and transcribed testimony (1991).

17. Gain control of fluency on the witness stand by speaking slowly, stressing syllables, easing into your breath pattern, and varying the loudness of your speech (1991).

18. Never accept the learned treatise as expertise unless you are master of it (1991).

19. Listen with care to the wording of the attorneys' questions and use this knowledge in the interests of precision and control (1991).

20. When the time is right to disagree with cross-examination questions, do so with strength, clarity, and conviction (1991).

21. Effective witnesses are familiar with expected trial procedures, interpersonal transactions, and the dynamics of testifying (1991).

22. Cross-examining attorneys will use substantive and psychological means to gain control over witnesses. Witnesses, in turn, need to be free of such control to perform well and feel good about their testimony (1991).

continued

23. Take a breath and explicitly think about questions that require thought (1991).

24. Look at the jury during narrative answers and avoid being captured in eye contact by the cross-examining attorney (1991).

25. Make the courtroom environment familiar and create an opportunity for control by sitting tall and owning personal space (1991).

26. If you do not know primary sources, worry not. Instead, stay with current knowledge and clinical conclusions (1991).

27. Cross-examination probes for guilt and shame are effective only if you respond with guilt and shame. Stay on-task and non-defensive (1991).

28. Talented professional witnesses can model authoritative expertise for other experts (1991).

29. When the cross-examination question is true but is asked in a pushy and negative manner, consider agreeing strongly (1991).

30. Quiet times on the stand can be used to observe carefully, stretch personal limits, and incorporate successes (1991).

31. Know the names and faces of the attorneys, judge, and other participants in the courtroom events (1991).

32. Both the teeming masses and esteemed scientific standards cross-examinations should be met with a comfortable affirmation of accepted and meaningful standards of practice (1991).

33. A witness's self-centeredness about the importance of personal testimony can serve as blinders that interfere with clarity, self-assurance, and non-defensiveness (1991).

34. Key moments can positively and negatively transform the credibility and acceptance of testimony (1991).

35. Dress for court in clothes that are familiar, comfortable, and professional (1991).

36. Make the last impression a good one (1991).

37. When lawyers fuss, stay uninvolved (1991).

38. Do not allow your reports or testimony to be recast into simple-minded and arbitrary groupings of the attorney's choice (1999).

continued

39. When the court limits what you can explain, neither panic nor become angry or defensive; rather, testify as confidently and accurately as you can within those constraints (1999).

40. Self-critical judgments and zealous attachment to the results distract from effective testimony. Seek to become authentically yourself as a professional and as a witness (1999).

41. Never make up answers, keep your answers carefully within the context of what you know and remember, and never automatically reply within attorneys' frames of reference (1999).

42. When minor gaps are questioned, answer matter-of-factly, and in the context of the nature of psychological evaluations and the findings of the case (1999).

43. In the normal and inevitable moments of feeling pulled toward evasiveness, concentrate carefully, and answer the difficult question (1999).

44. Part of being a great witness is to be a great teacher on the witness stand, and being a great teacher is the result of concerted effort (1999).

44. Anticipate cross-examination efforts to portray essential elements of your testimony as worthless (1999).

45. In the difficult moments in which women are patronized on the witness stand, they may gain control by restating their status as doctors without being strident and within the context of the questioning (1999).

46. Do not construct illusory support for opinions or methods, and do not be intimidated by such illusory constructions by attorneys (1999).

47. Inflammatory questions are best answered with calm explanations that demonstrate a confident sense of professional competence. Don't heat up on the stand (1999).

48. When confronted with your own fanciful and playful remarks, place them in context as fanciful and playful. (1999).

49. Whether it indeed would be nicer if one were not on the stand comes powerfully from the sense of shunning imposed by the

continued

attorneys and the witness's own internal self-assessments. Our transient self-judgments in response can be shaped and aided by experience and successes (1999).

50. Listen well: To ward off language viruses, you need to be "much, much better" at discerning meaning of words and phrases (1999).

51. When the attorney comments on one's testimony, having the "last word" can empower the witness and reduce a sense of helplessness (1999).

52. Avoid anti-lawyer jokes and quips on the witness stand. They are high-risk comments, to be reserved for rare and exactly fitting moments (1999).

53. Hostile attacks on one's character are best met with clear affirmations of worth and restatements of the essential issues (1999).

54. Flagrantly offensive language never has to be met passively. Options include going to the judge, recording the statement, confronting the speaker, consulting with colleagues, withdrawing from the case, or using the information as part of one's testimony (1999).

55. Scholarly preparation, composure, and negative assertions are preferred responses to personal attacks (1999).

56. Maintaining integrity on the stand calls for careful listening, avoidance of anticipatory answers, and staying faithful to your findings and knowledge (1999).

57. Pulling in a push-pull exchange is an art that requires non-defensive responding and meaningful practice (1999).

58. Witnesses are not obliged to answer all questions that appear to be related to their fields. Instead, witnesses need to attend to the direct applicability of the question and the extent to which the substance truly falls within their expertise (1999).

59. Questions about allegations of misconduct should be met forthrightly, indignantly, and openly (1999).

60. Rather than feeling disempowered by the absence of visual cues in telephone and videotape testimony, seek by practice and training to master your performance in the medium (1999).

continued

61. Address fears of crying and fainting on the stand by habituating to the courtroom, by drawing on an ally, by gaining perspective, and by calling for a break in your testimony, if necessary (1999).

62. Attorneys' pursuit of trivial topics during depositions is neither a cause for catastrophizing nor concern. Answer without suspiciousness as much as you can without jeopardizing the limits of your expertise (1999).

63. Decide for yourself what it is you dislike in yourself as an expert and what you like. Then, take active steps to diminish the aspects that do not work and enhance the ones that do (1999).

64. Fear and excessive self-conscientiousness are the natural enemies of good testimony. Preparation and realistic knowledge are the natural allies (2004).

65. Do not make automatic, aggressive, controlling yang replies to all aggressive questioning. Use some calmer, simpler, receptivey in responses (2004).

66. Use imagery as a tool to gain a sense of familiarity with the courtroom in order to ease anxiety and enhance your narrative style. Seek to feel positively connected to the people in the courtroom and to the physical place itself (2004).

67. Witnesses may choose to reverse the customary process in which attorneys set conceptual or linguistic traps for them. Such reversals should be offered only in the context of thorough preparation and consistent testimony (2004).

68. How you position and align yourself on the witness stand influences how your testimony will be received. Seek directed feedback on the direction of your body and positioning of your head while listening and while speaking in the courtroom (2004).

69. Unless you have had a remarkably good record of testifying in court, seek out witness preparation advice and video feedback to promote awareness, effectiveness, and credibility (2004).

70. Do not overdo it by trying very hard to speak correctly and properly on the stand, and do not overuse "I think," "I believe," and other personal references (2004).

continued

71. Pretentiousness is endemic to professional work. Check whether and how pretentiousness may impair your credibility on the stand, and enlist the aid of an insightful colleague to change it (2004).

72. High quality in expert methodology and opinions must be accompanied by effective delivery to make a difference. Do not be seen as overconfident (2004).

73. Avoid being a smug witness by acknowledging that you do not know everything, have not done everything, and are constructively willing to address more-of-everything questions (2004).

74. Check whether any aspects of your behaviors, appearance, or gestures make jurors suspicious, and if they do, seek to eliminate those aspects (2004).

75. Displays of emotions should be moderate, should be consistent with one's natural style, and should fit with the context about which one is testifying (2004).

76. Visceral images and sensationalistic questions may be met best with attentiveness and honesty, as well as professional detachment mixed with moderated empathy (2004).

77. Do not repeat the same phrases and words without a clear purpose; otherwise, your testimony may appear to slide into a style that seems automatic or evasive (2004).

78. Tailor your preparation for testimony to build on your strengths and compensate for your weaknesses. Memorize what you can. For the gaps that exist in memory and organization, invest heavily in preparing written outlines and memory aids before going to court (2004).

79. Never assume that you are beyond the reach of situational pulls that may distort your testimony. Stay alert to and resist the courtroom pulls to overstate credentials and findings. When possible, review transcripts of your own testimony as a check of your accuracy (2004).

80. Attorneys may chastise or corner witnesses during cross-examinations. Good witnesses stay effective and in control through simple, reflective, or method-oriented answers that come out of purposeful knowledge of attorney techniques (2004).

continued

81. Like all bullies, bullying attorneys look for vulnerabilities and depend on witnesses to be intimidated. Handle bullying questions by practicing and mastering interpersonal strength and professional poise under fire (2004).

82. Do not become ruffled when sensitive personal questions are asked, but rather stay controlled, factual, and non-defensive. Consider looking into possible ethical violations by the attorney as an absolute last resort (2004).

83. Gender-intrusive questions should be turned away with statements of privacy and clarification of the professional foundations of findings and testimony. If coerced to reply, keep answers minimal (2004).

84. In the rare event that you feel physically threatened on the stand, do not passively accept it. Intervene actively to get the assistance of the judge or others (2004).

85. One should make the best of being called to testify on short notice with little opportunity to prepare. Be honest, seek to be confident about the limitations of your knowledge, and allow your manner to transcend your uncertainties (2004).

86. Keep testimony coolly descriptive about your behaviors and about the litigants, when you may be excessively empathic or emotional about the case. Otherwise, allow modest degrees of empathic expression and limited personal feelings to appear in your testimony in order to be real and human about the issues (2004).

87. In small communities, ethical boundaries are often troublesome. Experts should have their policies about retention responsibly defined well in advance of being retained (2004).

88. One cannot seek out appointments on expert panels, but when it happens, it can be a learning opportunity in consensus and autonomy, insulated from customary adversarial events (2004).

89. Be emotionally prepared for the possibility that some of your answers will be limited to yes or no, but also be cognitively prepared to make the case that a yes or no answer is simply inadequate for the nature of the testimony (2004).

continued

90. Misleading echoes of experts' statements during cross-examinations may be met actively with confident restatements or passively by comfortable acceptance of the normal examination process (2004).

91. Do not permit interested parties or attorneys to coerce you into accepting interactions or assertions that are inconsistent with your expert role or findings (2004).

Substance vs. Style

Brodsky does not distinguish between substantive (what the expert says in testimony) and stylistic (how she says it) aspects of testimony. For several reasons, we find it useful to do so. (We use this as a convenient heuristic only; to our knowledge, only Heilbrun (2001) has previously applied this categorization to Brodsky's maxims.)

First, this distinction illustrates the value of both substance and style in expert testimony. Style without substance in expert testimony is poorly informed and misleading. But substance with little attention to stylistic influences—testimony by experts who have conducted careful, thorough, relevant evaluations but do not present these findings clearly, confidently, and credibly—is also less effective than it could be. This is consistent with the observation (Grisso, 1986) that *face validity*, the weakest form of validity in behavioral science research, is actually one of the most important in legal contexts. If the legal decision maker does not consider the evidence seriously because of how it is presented, it does not matter very much how substantively strong it might be.

Second, we use the substance/style distinction because it sharply delineates how the forensic clinician might prepare for expert testimony. Brodsky's substantive maxims clearly link the evaluation that was conducted (as described also by Simon and Gold, 2004(a); Melton et al., 2007; and Heilbrun, 2001) with the testimony that will be delivered. It is very difficult to imagine that testimony would be consistent with many of Brodsky's substantive maxims if this testimony were based on an evaluation that is insufficient, irrelevant, or intrusive. Forensic clinicians should attend carefully to the variety of stylistic maxims described by Brodsky—but only after having conducted an evaluation that is consistent with other aspects of FMHA best practice cited in this chapter and in the books that follow in this series.

Third, this distinction is useful because it helps forensic clinicians in training (and their supervisors) to conceptualize expert testimony as involving separate skill sets. The substantive skill set involves the integration of law, science, ethics, and practice into creating a sound evaluation, which is communicated in writing clearly and carefully. Stylistic skills, on the other hand, encompass the abilities to speak clearly, think efficiently and in a disciplined way (particularly when being challenged), and correct misperceptions that may arise from attempts to distort or change the intended meaning of one's testimony.

Major Themes

Brodsky's maxims involve an extraordinary condensation of complex considerations into brief, clear recommendations. Reviewing Table 4.5 yields three major themes, however—preparation, communication, and control—each of which encompass a number of different maxims.

PREPARATION

The importance of preparation is stressed very strongly. This comes through most clearly in a single maxim: "Overprepare: As in marriage, personal complacency can keep you from coping effectively with courtroom strife" (Brodsky, 1999, p. 62). However, a number of other maxims emphasize the importance of different aspects of preparation: checking one's own pattern of previous opinions and the impact of one's personal style, reviewing the literature in specific areas, communicating with relevant scholars in the field for clarification, being able to provide support for one's theories and methods in the face of a *Daubert* challenge, meeting with the attorney prior to testimony, providing the presenting attorney with a list of qualifying questions, being "culture educated," and mastering the foundations of expert knowledge and roles. All of these points are in addition to preparing to discuss the specific FMHA one has conducted in detail. This underscores a vital consideration for FMHA best practice: often, there is no substitute for hard work.

COMMUNICATION

The second theme involves communication. Since these maxims focus on giving testimony, they apply to oral communication rather than report-writing. Certainly the expert testimony provided in depositions, hearings, and trials should be based upon the written report when the full evaluation has been conducted. But there is a variety of ways in which experts can communicate more effectively in a courtroom, some of which go beyond describing the evaluation. Brodsky offers both substantive and stylistic maxims to facilitate effective communication in expert testimony. It can be particularly challenging to implement these maxims in cross-examination. These maxims focus on elements of communication that include eye contact, body posture, speech pattern, and breath control. They invoke the possibility of modeling one's style on that of an individual who is particularly skilled in this kind of communication. They emphasize the role of teaching, and avoiding the perception of smugness, overconfidence, hostility, or gratuitous humor. Taken together, these maxims identify a series of steps to take (and others to avoid) that offer a disciplined approach to communicating as an expert.

CONTROL

The third theme is control: both establishing it and regaining it when it is lost. Brodsky envisions expert testimony as occurring in the midst of a symbolic battle. The vigorous challenge to one's data and conclusions from opposing counsel should be anticipated, but maintaining one's poise and continuing to think and speak clearly in the midst of such cross-examination is one of the most difficult aspects of expert testimony. These maxims provide a variety of steps that may be helpful. Some incorporate suggested responses to extreme tactics such as sensitive personal questions, gender-intrusiveness, or having a screwdriver placed near the witness's throat. Others anticipate the more routine ways in which cross-examining attorneys may attempt to challenge the expert's data, reasoning, or conclusions. They acknowledge an important purpose of cross-examination as exposing any weaknesses of expert testimony that is unsound, inaccurate, or irrelevant—but advise the expert whose testimony is sound how it best may be presented over the course of the entire cross-examination.

Conclusion

These maxims are drawn from the professional practice literature. Some have independent empirical support, but no investigator has yet considered them as a body and asked the obvious research question: Does adhering to these maxims enhance the quality of expert testimony? This will clearly be important for the field in years to come. At present, these maxims exist as a series of wise conclusions drawn by a creative scholar and experienced forensic psychologist, greatly enhanced by the collective experience of others who have written to him, taken his workshops, sought his advice, and in turn provided accounts of their own experiences in court.

Principles of FMHA: An Integration

The maxims, guidelines, and principles described in this chapter have been written at differing levels of specificity and by different disciplines. At this point, it is useful to revisit the question posed early in this chapter: Are there broad, foundational principles applicable to FMHA of different kinds? In light of the information presented thus far in this chapter, we can clearly answer this question affirmatively. Furthermore, we can integrate these various attempts at describing broadly applicable aspects of FMHA into a set of principles that appears to represent the most contemporary views of the nature of such principles.

This integrated list of FMHA principles may be seen in Table 4.6. This list was developed by starting with the principles described by Heilbrun (2001), which represent the work most clearly focused on describing such foundational principles. We have expanded and modified these principles in light of the work that has appeared since 2001, particularly considering the contributions of Simon and Gold, Melton et al., and Brodsky described in this chapter.

Our discussion in this section will focus on principles that have been added or changed. Principles that are largely unchanged have been described earlier in Chapter 3 and in this chapter. Our first step in amending and integrating principles involved adding a "General" section that does not apply to any particular case. There are seven principles in this general section (see Table 4.6)

Table 4.6 Principles of Forensic Mental Health Assessment:
An Integration

GENERALLY

1. Be aware of the important differences between clinical and forensic domains.
2. Obtain appropriate education, training, and experience in one's area of forensic specialization.
3. Be familiar with the relevant legal, ethical, scientific, and practice literatures pertaining to FMHA.
4. Be guided by honesty and striving for impartiality, actively disclosing the limitations on as well as the support for one's opinions.
5. Control potential evaluator bias in general through monitoring case selection, continuing education, and consultation with knowledgeable colleagues.
6. Be familiar with specific aspects of the legal system, particularly communication, discovery, deposition, and testimony.
7. Do not become adversarial, but present and defend your opinions effectively.

IN SPECIFIC CASES
PREPARATION

8. Identify relevant forensic issues.
9. Accept referrals only within area of expertise.
10. Decline the referral when evaluator impartiality is unlikely.
11. Clarify the evaluator's role with the attorney.
12. Clarify financial arrangements.
13. Obtain appropriate authorization.
14. Avoid playing the dual roles of therapist and forensic evaluator.

continued

15. Determine the particular role to be played within forensic assessment if the referral is accepted.

16. Select the most appropriate model to guide data gathering, interpretation, and communication.

DATA COLLECTION

17. Use multiple sources of information for each area being assessed. Review the available background information and actively seek important missing elements.

18. Use relevance and reliability (validity) as guides for seeking information and selecting data sources.

19. Obtain relevant historical information.

20. Assess clinical characteristics in relevant, reliable, and valid ways.

21. Assess legally relevant behavior.

22. Ensure that conditions for evaluation are quiet, private, and distraction-free.

23. Provide appropriate notification of purpose and/or obtain appropriate authorization before beginning.

24. Determine whether the individual understands the purpose of the evaluation and the associated limits on confidentiality.

DATA INTERPRETATION

25. Use third party information in assessing response style.

26. Use testing when indicated in assessing response style.

27. Use case-specific (idiographic) evidence in assessing clinical condition, functional abilities, and causal connection.

28. Use nomothetic evidence is assessing clinical condition, functional abilities, and causal connection.

29. Use scientific reasoning in assessing causal connection between clinical condition and functional abilities.

30. Carefully consider whether to answer the ultimate legal question. If it is answered, it should be in the context of a thorough evaluation

continued

clearly describing data and reasoning, and with the clear recognition that this question is in the domain of the legal decision maker.

31. Describe findings and limits so that they need change little under cross examination.

WRITTEN COMMUNICATION

32. Attribute information to sources.

33. Use plain language; avoid technical jargon.

34. Write report in sections, according to model and procedures.

TESTIMONY

35. Base testimony on the results of the properly performed FMHA.

36. Prepare.

37. Communicate effectively.

38. Control the message. Strive to obtain, retain, and regain control over the meaning and impact of what is presented in expert testimony.

General Principles

BE AWARE OF THE IMPORTANT DIFFERENCES BETWEEN CLINICAL AND FORENSIC DOMAINS

This is a very important consideration for individuals with training in clinical service delivery who also sub-specialize in forensic assessment. It is discussed by various contributors to the Simon and Gold volume, by Melton et al., and by Heilbrun and colleagues. Refer back to Table 4.3 for a summary of such differences.

OBTAIN APPROPRIATE EDUCATION, TRAINING, AND EXPERIENCE IN ONE'S AREA OF FORENSIC SPECIALIZATION

Various reflections of specialty training have been discussed in Chapter 2 and Chapter 3 of the book, including forensic fellowships and continuing professional education, with forensic board certification an indication of such specialization that integrates education, training, and experience with demonstrated knowledge and skills. If formal training opportunities in forensic psychology and forensic psychiatry continue to expand, there may be a growing expectation that forensic specialization will be attained through formal training. But this principle stresses the important link between education, training, and experience as a means to develop FMHA competence and the nature of that particular competence and how it is used. Moreover, the forensic clinician should be fully prepared to describe how his competence in FMHA was developed, and the basis for his expertise.

BE FAMILIAR WITH THE RELEVANT LEGAL, ETHICAL, SCIENTIFIC, AND PRACTICE LITERATURES PERTAINING TO FMHA

These four domains are primary sources of authority in FMHA (see Chapter 3). The knowledge they impart must be applied in specific cases, as is emphasized in the discussion of the principles described by Heilbrun (2001) earlier in this chapter. However, these sources—apart from their important application to individual cases—also provide a broad base of information that any competent forensic clinician must have reviewed, considered, and integrated into her overall approach to FMHA.

BE GUIDED BY HONESTY AND STRIVING FOR IMPARTIALITY, ACTIVELY DISCLOSING THE LIMITATIONS ON, AS WELL AS THE SUPPORT FOR, ONE'S OPINIONS

This is a variation of a guideline that appears in the *Ethical Guidelines for the Practice of Forensic Psychiatry*. It applies comparably well to forensic clinicians who are not psychiatrists. The word *impartiality* is used instead of *objectivity* because the former better conveys the active attempt to recognize and limit possible evaluator bias. One way for the forensic clinician to do so is by conveying opinions for which limitations and inconsistent data are actively disclosed.

CONTROL POTENTIAL EVALUATOR BIAS IN GENERAL THROUGH MONITORING CASE SELECTION, CONTINUING EDUCATION, AND CONSULTATION WITH KNOWLEDGEABLE COLLEAGUES

Consistent with the previous principle, there are broad, general approaches to managing potential bias as well as those that are specific to certain kinds of cases. An overview of the cases the forensic clinician accepts, as well as ensuring that there are opportunities to discuss recurring or troubling influences with colleagues, and reading or hearing what others say on this topic, are important general approaches to managing bias that need not be associated with any specific case.

BE FAMILIAR WITH THE SPECIFIC ASPECTS OF THE LEGAL SYSTEM, PARTICULARLY COMMUNICATION, DISCOVERY, DEPOSITION, AND TESTIMONY

An earlier principle in this section stressed the importance of knowing relevant law. This principle is more specific. There are particular procedures with which a forensic clinician must be familiar, ranging from formal and informal communication with attorneys, evidentiary standards regarding evidence that is exchanged by opposing counsels, the less formal discovery and the more formal testimony at hearing or trial. Such familiarity allows the forensic clinician to make appropriate requests and responses, and to avoid pitfalls that could result from insufficient awareness of the nature of such basic legal procedures.

DO NOT BECOME ADVERSARIAL, BUT PRESENT AND DEFEND YOUR OPINIONS EFFECTIVELY

This can involve a precarious balancing act. In an adversarial system in which opposing attorneys engage in conflict that is more than symbolic, it can be very difficult to avoid being drawn into the battle. Nonetheless, it is crucial for the forensic clinician, who must be guided by the need for honesty and relative impartiality, to strike the balance that effectively presents one's data and opinions but regards that—rather than winning—as the goal.

Revised Principles

In addition to these general principles, we have revised several of the existing principles described by Heilbrun (2001). Principle #17 in Table 4.6 reflects the addition of a second sentence that goes beyond the assertion that the evaluator should use "multiple sources of information for each area being assessed" to refer to the materials (such as discovery) that are provided to the evaluator. There may be gaps in this information. When there are, the forensic clinician is encouraged to identify them and actively seek the important missing elements.

The principle in Table 4.6 concerning ultimate issue testimony has also been amended. A straightforward ban on ever answering the ultimate legal question is not consistent with our earlier discussion in Chapter 3. However, we can specify certain conditions that are consistent with best practice if the forensic clinician does choose to answer the ultimate question. First, this answer should occur in the larger context of having provided a thorough evaluation, with data and reasoning clearly communicated, so the legal consumer (if she chooses) could separate such data and reasoning from the additional political and moral values embedded in ultimate legal questions. Second, the report or testimony should include a reminder that the forensic clinician is aware that ultimate legal questions are the domain of the court, not the evaluator, perhaps by using certain language (e.g., "it is my clinical opinion that the defendant is competent to stand trial") to underscore this distinction.

Finally, in the principles on expert testimony, one principle ("testify effectively") has been dropped. In its place we have substituted three principles:

PREPARE

This applies both to one's preparation for translating the results of the FMHA report into testimony on direct examination, and to anticipating how it might be challenged on cross-examination. It is a crucial reminder that there is no easy, straightforward path to excellence. Like conducting the evaluation, there is a good deal of work that goes into effective expert testimony—and much of it is performed before the expert steps onto the witness stand.

COMMUNICATE EFFECTIVELY

There are both substantive and stylistic contributions to communicating one's meaning effectively. Both must be recognized and respected. Although an earlier principle underscores the importance of using the FMHA report (in turn reflecting the data and reasoning from the full evaluation) as a platform for testimony, it can be challenging to do so even on direct examination. Cross-examination can be far more difficult, as the expert copes simultaneously with conveying meaning and handling challenges intended to change how such communication is understood.

CONTROL THE MESSAGE

Strive to obtain, retain, and regain control over the meaning and impact of what is presented in expert testimony.

This principle applies almost exclusively to cross-examination, and how effectively the expert can continue to convey his findings while under vigorous, multifaceted challenge. Obtaining and keeping sufficient control to do so, or regaining that control when it is temporarily lost, is the important capacity that he must master to implement this principle effectively.

These three principles have been distilled from the 153 expert-testimony maxims described by Brodsky (1991, 1999, 2004). It is impossible, using a small number of principles, to do justice to the complexity and nuances contained in these maxims. Nevertheless, these three principles do seem to capture a good deal of what Brodsky has offered in his aspirational description of effective expert testimony.

Conclusion

This chapter has addressed the roles of broad principles, and more specific guidelines and maxims, in helping to shape best practice in FMHA. There is a good deal of overlap in the broad principles (Heilbrun, 2001; Melton et al., 2007), guidelines (Simon & Gold, 2004a), and expert testimony maxims (Brodsky, 1991, 1999, 2004) we have presented. This is reassuring. The extent of their agreement provides a form of consensual validation for the broader, more theoretical aspects of FMHA best practice. It also allowed their integration into a revised, updated set of principles that applies to FMHA broadly.

Toward Best Practices in Forensic Mental Health Assessment | **5**

It would be presumptuous for mental health professionals or behavioral scientists to write a book (let alone a series) on the standard of care in FMHA in general. We distinguish between "standards of care" (which are enforceable legally), "standards of practice" (which may be enforceable under ethics codes), and "best practices" (which are aspirational). Defining the standard of care is the law's prerogative, typically done by the court, in a way that is *informed* but *not dictated* by evidence regarding standards of practice (Heilbrun et al., under review). Focusing on standards of practice would fall more within the expertise of the authors in this series. However, standard of practice in FMHA is a complex determination affected by multiple influences. These include (1) ethics codes applicable to the entire profession; (2) specialty guidelines developed to address more specialized forensic issues; (3) broad principles of FMHA; (4) meta-analyses or national surveys describing outcomes or practices; (5) descriptions of specialized forensic assessment instruments, including their psychometric properties and validation evidence; (6) books, chapters, courses, and continuing education workshops that inform broad aspects of practice in specific areas; and (7) single studies with particularly relevant data (Heilbrun et al., under review). The present book series will certainly provide information relevant to decisions about standards of practice. However, deciding on such standards must ultimately involve the broader field to a greater extent that any single book, or series of books, can hope to do.

The volumes in this series, therefore, focus on "best practices" in FMHA. Development of the series has required careful scrutiny of existing ethical, legal, scientific, and practice literature by authors selected for their specific expertise, followed by review by series editors and outside experts. The series' objective is to produce volumes that will inform practitioners, trainees, students, legal consumers, policy-makers, and forensic administrators about the highest level of practice that is feasible in the areas addressed in this series.

This final chapter describes the process of "standard setting" in more detail. Then it describes the basic structure for all books in the series, and finally it describes the topics and summarizes the contributions of each of the remaining 19 books in this FMHA best-practice series.

Establishing Standards for Forensic Mental Health Assessment

Standards of practice for a field can be of several kinds. Some standards express a minimally acceptable level of performance. They identify features of practice that must be achieved, with failure to do so being considered "unacceptable" practice. These are the kind of standards applied in tort litigation in which the question involves whether a professional has met the "standard of care." Other standards describe desirable practice, detailing an approach that professionals should strive to achieve and can typically be met. We think of these as comparable to "standards of practice." Finally, there is a third category, composed of standards that express "best practice." They represent practice at its best, given the available theories, methods, and procedures in the field. Performance that meets a best-practice standard is achieved only sometimes, even by the most accomplished practitioners. Circumstances of specific cases often do not allow one to engage in practices that reach this standard. In this sense, best-practice standards are clearly aspirational. One uses them as a model or guide, recognizing that only sometimes will one's performance fulfill the standard.

Purpose of This Series

This book series will offer *best-practice standards* for the 19 types of FMHA that the volumes address. This has several implications for how the volumes should be read and used. They do not establish a required standard of practice for forensic mental health evaluations.

Attorneys who question clinicians about their forensic practice should not expect to be able to use these standards as though they were requirements for forensic practice, or as though clinicians not meeting these standards are practicing incompetently or inappropriately. Each volume does describe unacceptable practices. But the series' main purpose is to describe a hypothetical best practice that often exceeds our ability in specific cases. A best-practice standard recognizes a considerable amount of territory between "unacceptable" practices and "best" practices, and striving within that territory to aspire to the higher objective constitutes "acceptable" practice.

Limits of Best-Practice Standards

Developing and using best-practice standards for FMHA should be undertaken with an awareness of the limitations of such standards.

CONSENSUS

First, when expressions of standards for a field are at their best, they represent a consensus of those who protect, guide, and nurture the field. Who those protectors are, or should be, has no clear definition, however. Sometimes they are a few authorities with senior status, and occasionally they are a committee of experts identified as such by their peers. However they are constituted, they will agree on some points and disagree on others. Where there are disagreements, the best that can be done is to be aware of alternative viewpoints so that one can explain to others the sources of controversy. As a result, any definition of best practice in a field is far less than an absolute and infallible dictum. It is an invention that results from a group's effort to aspire to a meaningful consensus of the field. That means that at least some professionals in a field—even its greater authorities—may differ on some of the specifics of a standard.

The standards expressed in this series were authored by respected experts with national reputations in their subfields of FMHA. Their initial manuscripts were reviewed by at least two of the editors of the series. They were then reviewed by several experts in the author's specific area of FMHA, each of whom has many years of experience contributing to national FMHA standard-setting activities and credentialing of forensic mental health professionals. This review process and the authors' revisions in response to reviewer comments represent the series' effort to achieve a reasonable consensus regarding best practice.

SHELF-LIFE

A second limitation of best-practice standards is that they have a shelf-life. As a dynamic ideal, standards of practice are always changing as a consequence of advances in the scientific base for the field and scholarly debate about issues of practice. A published standard of practice, therefore, is always decaying in relation to the dynamic evolution of the field. The length of a published standard's shelf-life depends in part on how rapidly the field advances, which is often difficult to predict. Moreover, broad principles to guide the assessment process are likely to change less rapidly than, for example, recommendations regarding specific assessment tools. The present series of best-practice volumes adjusts to this limitation with its intention to provide online updates as needed, as well as potential publication of second editions further in the future if the volumes prove helpful to the field.

APPLICATION TO DIVERSE CASES AND CIRCUMSTANCES

A third limitation of best-practice standards is in their application to diverse cases and circumstances. Some examiners work in busy metropolitan centers and large courts, while others practice in greater isolation as they offer a dozen rural courts their only source of forensic evaluations. Some are state-employed, and others are in private practice. Some work in states with statutes that absolutely require an "ultimate expert opinion," while others regularly testify before judges who forbid it. Some examiners work in services that are able to hire technicians to obtain necessary medical and school records for their evaluations within a few days, while others have neither the resources nor the authority to get records in less than a month. Legal definitions of the forensic questions that they address may differ from one state to another, and judicial demands may differ between courts within the same state. Forensic psychologists and forensic psychiatrists may face different laws controlling their practice even within a common state. Developing a single set of best practices for two different professions in a nation with 51 sets of laws is a daunting task. The success with which this can be done depends largely on recognizing specifically how jurisdictions and professions may differ, then crafting the standard in a manner that accommodates that diversity rather than offering a rigid set of rules.

Structure and Content of Each of the Remaining Nineteen Volumes

There is no single way to organize standards for best practice. For this series, the editors developed an organizational scheme that is applied uniformly across volumes, despite the diversity of the areas of FMHA that they cover. Table 5.1 lists the volumes in this series. The topics for 17 of the 19 volumes were selected to represent what the series editors considered to be the most important and oft-considered legal questions in which forensic clinicians assist legal decision makers. The other two topics—jury selection and eyewitness testimony—are not addressed by forensic clinicians. Instead, they are considered in the course of legal proceedings by consultants specializing in these topics and providing relevant information to courts and attorneys.

Series Template

Each volume has seven chapters describing essential principles, knowledge, and practice recommendations for the volume's specific type of FMHA:

- *Legal Context:* How the forensic question is structured by its sociolegal purpose, legal standards, and legal procedures

- *Forensic Mental Health Concepts:* Principles and methods for translating the legal question into psycholegal questions that are amenable to assessment

- *Empirical Foundations and Limits:* Knowing the scientific theories and research results that can guide conceptualization and practice in FMHA in the area in question, and that identify the limits of scientific or clinical expertise

- *Preparation for the Evaluation:* Recognizing procedural and ethical issues in developing and implementing the assessment plan

Table 5.1	Titles in the Series BEST PRACTICES IN FORENSIC MENTAL HEALTH ASSESSMENT

Foundations of Forensic Mental Health Assessment

Criminal Titles:

Evaluation of Competence to Stand Trial

Evaluation of Criminal Responsibility

Evaluation of Capacity to Confess

Evaluation of Sexually Violent Predators

Evaluation for Risk of Violence in Adults

Jury Selection

Evaluation for Capital Sentencing

Eyewitness Identification

Civil Titles:

Evaluation of Capacity to Consent to Treatment

Evaluation for Substituted Judgment

Evaluation for Personal Injury Claims

Evaluation for Civil Commitment

Evaluation for Harassment and Discrimination Claims

Evaluation of Workplace Disability

Juvenile and Family Titles:

Evaluation for Child Custody

Evaluation of Juveniles' Competence to Stand Trial

Evaluation for Risk of Violence in Juveniles

Evaluation for Child Protection

Evaluation for Disposition and Transfer of Juvenile Offenders

- *Data Collection:* Descriptions of best practices regarding data collection instruments and procedures

- *Interpretation:* Recognizing the form and substance of interpretations of data, so that opinions maximize one's capacities but remain within the limits of what the state of the art will allow

- *Report Writing and Testimony:* Strategies for organizing reports and deciding what needs to be reported, and how to express various aspects of FMHA results in a manner that maximizes others' understanding of it

Specific Volumes

The following descriptions of each of the volumes proceeds from criminal to civil to juvenile/family forensic topics, although volumes in the series—to be published across a three-year period—will not be published in this sequence.

EVALUATION OF COMPETENCE TO STAND TRIAL

One of the most commonly raised clinical-legal issues for criminal defendants is competence to stand trial (sometimes called "competence to proceed" or "adjudicative competence"). Defendants cannot be tried if they do not have the capacity to understand and participate in their defense. If they cannot, and if the cause of their incapacity is mental illness or mental retardation, they must be restored to competency before the trial can proceed. If they cannot be restored, then different jurisdictions call for various dispositions, including dismissal of charges and civil commitment. Competence to stand trial evaluations require careful assessment of the individual's relevant functional abilities and clinical conditions.

EVALUATION OF CRIMINAL RESPONSIBILITY

A criminal defendant's mental state at the time of the offense is an important but complex and challenging form of FMHA. Since this kind of evaluation is "reconstructive," or focused on a defendant's mental state at a previous time, it requires gauging that individual's relevant thinking, feeling, and behavior when the erosion of memory may limit the accuracy of accounts given by the defendant and third party observers.

EVALUATION OF CAPACITY TO CONFESS

Many criminal defendants are convicted on the basis of inculpatory statements given to police during custodial interrogation. But such statements may be excluded if the court determines that they were not given in a knowing, intelligent, and voluntary fashion by the defendant. The challenge of assessing whether the statement was delivered in a knowing and intelligent way (about which forensic clinicians have a good deal to offer) or in a voluntary fashion (about which forensic clinicians have less to say, although they may be able to comment on the impact of the interrogators' behavior on evaluee decision making) is addressed in this volume. This volume will also consider issues related to the assessment of the truthfulness of confessions offered by defendants, including the limits of such opinions.

EVALUATION OF SEXUALLY VIOLENT PREDATORS

There are three points in the criminal process that involve a specialized decision for convicted sexual offenders: at sentencing (when a defendant may receive an enhanced sentence if designated by the court as a "sexually violent predator"), following the end of sentence (when a defendant may be civilly committed to a specialized facility for sexual offenders), and upon return to the community (the process of which may involve designated steps, including public notification). The primary focus in this volume will be the third of these areas.

EVALUATION FOR RISK OF VIOLENCE IN ADULTS

The practice of violence risk assessment has changed dramatically in the last two decades. With the development of specialized risk assessment tools and a greatly enhanced empirical foundation, forensic clinicians can now conduct evaluations that are conceptually sharper and empirically stronger. Risk assessment, unlike most other topics in this series, is not itself an ultimate legal question for the courts to decide. But it is embedded in a variety of other topics, including civil commitment, juvenile commitment, and sentencing in specialized contexts (e.g., sexual offender, capital punishment). The challenge of disentangling this overlap, as well as describing specialized tools and relevant empirical support, will be undertaken in this volume.

JURY SELECTION

The process of selecting a jury can be quite important in the early stages of a trial. Providing useful and accurate information to attorneys, however, requires knowledge and experience unlike that needed to provide evaluations in most other areas covered by this series. The jury selection consultation process will be described within a structure comparable to the other volumes, and "best practice" in consultation in light of the relevant research and other sources of authority will be addressed.

EVALUATION FOR CAPITAL SENTENCING

The stakes are enormous when a judge or jury must decide whether a defendant, convicted of a capital offense, should receive the death penalty. The need for "best practice" is enhanced in such a context, when the cost of error is so high. Forensic clinicians who conduct evaluations that contribute to capital sentencing decisions will be guided by reading this volume; attorneys and judges can get a better sense of the goals to which such evaluators should aspire in conducting a thorough, multi-sourced, and accurate evaluation in a capital context.

EYEWITNESS IDENTIFICATION

The accuracy of eyewitness accounts is an important aspect of legal proceedings, particularly in criminal areas, and has been studied extensively by behavioral scientists. Best-practice standards for consultation to courts and attorneys on the topic of eyewitness identification will be addressed in this volume.

EVALUATION OF CAPACITY TO CONSENT TO TREATMENT

The capacity to consent to treatment is an issue that may arise in the course of civil commitment proceedings (in which a "voluntary" patient must have such capacity; see *Zinermon v. Burch,* 1990). It is also a question that must be addressed by any treatment team working with a hospitalized patient who declines some aspect of recommended treatment. If such an individual has the needed capacity to consent to (and decline) treatment, then the treatment team can override this decision only through legally recognized avenues. For an individual without such capacity, however, the team may have the option of seeking a substituted judgment through appointment of a third party.

This volume will also include an additional chapter on competence to consent to research. There is a certain overlap between the constructs of competence to consent to treatment and competence to consent to research, which is why they will appear in the same volume. However, they are also sufficiently different that it is better to include the latter in one final, single chapter rather than interweaving the two throughout the book.

EVALUATION FOR SUBSTITUTED JUDGMENT

Questions involving the need for substituted judgment can arise in a variety of legal contexts. One example is involuntary hospitalization in the context of capacity to consent to treatment, noted in the description of Volume 10. Others include different legal decisions in the areas of contracts, financial commitments, medical decision-making, independent and supervised living, and testamentary capacity.

EVALUATION FOR PERSONAL INJURY CLAIMS

Personal injury litigation can be very complex, underscoring the importance of conceptual accuracy as well as legal relevance and thoroughness in FMHA. To prevail in such litigation, a plaintiff must establish that the defendant breached a duty to the plaintiff, proximally causing harm and resulting in damages. Forensic clinicians conducting this kind of FMHA are asked to assess the nature, extent, and genuineness of damages—but must also assess whether and how the breach of the duty was related to observed injuries.

EVALUATION FOR CIVIL COMMITMENT

Civil commitment decisions are made often by courts in the United States, but the standards for FMHA in contributing to these decisions have not been high. Indeed, clinicians asked to evaluate an individual for the purpose of a civil commitment decision (initial or continued hospitalization) often limit their evaluation to a brief interview and the completion of a checklist. This volume will recognize the frequency of civil commitment decisions and the overly casual nature of FMHA evaluations that have contributed to it.

EVALUATION FOR HARASSMENT AND DISCRIMINATION CLAIMS

Employment discrimination and harassment is an area that has changed substantially during the last two decades. The complexity of legal standards is one challenge facing the forensic clinician; the reconstructive aspect of the impact of the employer's alleged conduct on the plaintiff is another. This volume will sort out the legal complexities and practical challenges in describing a best-practice standard for FMHA in this area.

EVALUATION OF WORKPLACE DISABILITY

The question of whether an individual has become disabled from mental, emotional, or cognitive problems to the extent that she can no longer work is an important one. It may be requested by an insurance company checking the current status of an individual who is receiving disability benefits. It may also arise in the course of litigation involving the insured individual and the company providing benefits. Important questions include the nature and severity of symptoms and their impact on functional demands such as capacities to work on a specific job—or perhaps any job. This volume will address best practice in this area.

EVALUATION FOR CHILD CUSTODY

There has been much debate about what forensic clinicians can provide in child custody evaluations. The question before the court is highly complex, involving the best custodial arrangement for divorcing parents with iterations that include physical custody, legal custody, and sole versus shared custody, all viewed through the lens of the best interests of the children involved.

EVALUATION OF JUVENILES' COMPETENCE TO STAND TRIAL

Juvenile competence to stand trial shares some important components with its adult counterpart, but there are important differences as well. Competence to stand trial in juvenile court is among the newest of forensic mental health assessments, having been virtually nonexistent in most juvenile courts 15 years ago. Some youth lack relevant capacities for competence to stand trial, not because of mental illness—as is traditionally the case in adult criminal cases—but because of developmental immaturity. In addition, there are many differences in the assessment of adults and adolescents in general, as well as differences in relevant psychopathology. Both the overlap (reliance on *Dusky* for the basic standard) and the distinctions (particularly the importance of developmental considerations and their impact on functional demands) will be described.

EVALUATION FOR RISK OF VIOLENCE IN JUVENILES

Assessing the risk of future violence in juveniles, like that in adults, is not a specific type of evaluation and not a legal question for courts by itself. However, it contributes substantially to decisions about need for pretrial detention, transfer to criminal court, and disposition (placement) after youth have been found delinquent. It is also an area that has enjoyed a substantial research focus during the last two decades, resulting in the development of specialized tools that can assist the forensic evaluator in assessing juvenile violence risk.

EVALUATION FOR CHILD PROTECTION

Child protection evaluations inform legal decisions concerning whether children are at risk for abuse or neglect at the hands of their caretakers. As in child custody evaluations, the forensic clinician must be guided by a primary concern for the child's well-being, but simultaneously maintain a respect for the rights of all others concerned as well. This volume will include a review of the issues related to assessments designed to provide information related to the termination of parental rights.

EVALUATION FOR COMMITMENT AND TRANSFER OF JUVENILE OFFENDERS

One of the most common decisions made by juvenile judges concerns whether a youth adjudicated delinquent should be committed for treatment in the community or in a more distant, secure, residential placement. Another decision, made with increasing frequency during the last decade, is whether a youth who is under 18 should be handled within the juvenile system or transferred to the criminal system to be processed as an adult. These decisions share a focus on the broad considerations of public safety and treatment needs and amenability. However, the particular evaluations in these areas conducted to assist either legal decision are complex, incorporating developmental considerations, risk assessment and risk management, and appraisal of likely response to different interventions.

References

American Academy of Child and Adolescent Psychiatry (1997). Practice parameters for child custody evaluation. *Journal of the American Academy of Child and Adolescent Psychiatry, 36,* 57S–68S.

American Academy of Child and Adolescent Psychiatry (1997). Practice parameters for the forensic evaluation of children and adolescents who may have been physically or sexually abused. *Journal of the American Academy of Child and Adolescent Psychiatry, 36,* 37S–56S.

American Academy of Child and Adolescent Psychiatry (1997). Practice parameters for the assessment and treatment of children and adolescents with conduct disorder. *Journal of the American Academy of Child and Adolescent Psychiatry, 36,* 122S–139S.

American Academy of Child and Adolescent Psychiatry (1998). Practice parameters for the assessment and treatment of children and adolescents with posttraumatic stress disorder. *Journal of the American Academy of Child and Adolescent Psychiatry, 37,* 997–1001.

American Academy of Child and Adolescent Psychiatry (1999). Practice parameters for the assessment and treatment of children and adolescents who are sexually abusive of others. *Journal of the American Academy of Child and Adolescent Psychiatry, 38,* 55S–76S.

American Academy of Psychiatry and the Law (2002). Practice guideline for forensic psychiatric evaluation of defendants raising the insanity defense. *Journal of the American Academy of Psychiatry and the Law, 30,* S1–S40.

American Academy of Psychiatry and the Law (2005). *Ethical guidelines for the practice of forensic psychiatry.* Bloomfield, CT: American Academy of Psychiatry and the Law.

American Psychiatric Association (2001). *The principles of medical ethics with annotation especially applicable to psychiatry.* Washington, D.C.: American Psychiatric Association.

American Psychological Association (2007). Record keeping guidelines. *American Psychologist, 62,* 993–1004.

American Psychological Association (1994). Guidelines for child custody evaluations in divorce proceedings. *American Psychologist, 49,* 677–680.

American Psychological Association (1999). Guidelines for psychological evaluations in child protection matters. *American Psychologist, 54,* 586–593.

American Psychological Association (2002a). Ethical principles of psychologists and code of conduct. *American Psychologist, 57,* 1060–1073.

American Psychological Association (2002b). *Guidelines on multicultural education, training, research practice, and organizational change for psychologists.* Washington, D.C.: American Psychological Association.

American Psychological Association (2006). Report of the ethics committee (2005). *American Psychologist, 61,* 522–529.

Appelbaum, P. (1997). A theory of ethics for forensic psychiatry. *Journal of the American Academy of Psychiatry and the Law, 25,* 233–247.

Appelbaum, P., & Gutheil, T. (1991). *Clinical handbook of psychiatry and the law* (2nd edition). Baltimore: Williams & Wilkins.

Appelbaum, P., & Gutheil, T. (2007). *Clinical handbook of psychiatry and the law* (4th edition). Baltimore: Lippincott, Williams & Wilkins.

Appelbaum, P., & Roth, L. (1982). Competency to consent to research: A psychiatric overview. *Archives of General Psychiatry, 39,* 951–958.

Appelbaum, P., Lidz, C., & Meisel, A. (1987). *Informed consent: Legal theory and clinical practice.* New York: Oxford University Press.

Ash, P. (2004). Children and adolescents. In R. Simon & L. Gold (Eds.), *Textbook of forensic psychiatry* (pp. 449–470). Washington, D.C.: American Psychiatric Publishing.

Association of Family and Conciliation Courts (2006). *Model standards of practice for child custody evaluation.* Milwaukee, WI: Author.

Bank, S. C., & Packer, I. K. (2007). Expert witness testimony: Law, ethics, and practice. In A. M. Goldstein (Ed.), *Forensic psychology: Emerging topics and expanding roles,* (pp. 421–445). Hoboken, NJ: John Wiley and Sons.

Barlow, D. H. (2005). What's new about evidenced-based assessment? *Psychological Assessment, 17,* 308–311.

Bartol, C., & Bartol, A. (2004). History of forensic psychology. In A. Hess & I. Weiner (Eds.), *Handbook of forensic psychology* (2nd edition) (pp. 3–23). New York: John Wiley.

Bersoff, D., Goodman-Delahunty, J., Grisso, T., Hans, V., Poythress, N., & Roesch, R. (1997). Training in law and psychology: Models from the Villanova Conference. *American Psychologist, 52,* 1301–1310.

Blau, T. H. (1984). *The psychologist as expert witness.* New York: Wiley.

Borum, R., Bartel, P., & Forth, A. (2003). *Manual for the Structured Assessment for Violence Risk in Youth (SAVRY): Version 1.1.* Tampa, FL: Louis de la Parte Florida Mental Health Institute, University of South Florida.

Borum, R., & Grisso, T. (1995). Psychological test use in criminal forensic evaluations. *Professional Psychology: Research and Practice, 26,* 465–473.

Borum, R., & Otto, R. (2000) Advances in forensic assessment and treatment. *Law and Human Behavior, 24,* 1–7.

Borum, R., & Verhaagen, D. (2006). *Assessing and managing violence risk in juveniles.* New York: Guilford.

Bradford, D. L. (2001). Dissecting Missouri's requirement of "reasonable medical certainty." *Journal of the Missouri Bar, 57,* 136–142.

Brakel, S. (1974). Presumption, bias, and incompetence in the criminal process. *Wisconsin Law Review,* pp. 1105–1130.

Brigham, J., & Grisso, T. (2003). Forensic psychology. In D. Freedheim (Ed.), *Handbook of Psychology: Volume 1, History of psychology* (pp. 391–411). Hoboken, NJ: John Wiley.

Brodsky, S. (1973). *Psychologists in the criminal justice system.* Urbana, IL: University of Illinois Press.

Brodsky, S. (1991). *Testifying in court: Guidelines and maxims for the expert witness.* Washington, D.C.: American Psychological Association.

Brodsky, S. (1999). *The expert expert witness: More maxims and guidelines for testifying in court.* Washington, D.C.: American Psychological Association.

Brodsky, S. (2004). *Coping with cross-examination and other pathways to effective testimony.* Washington, D.C.: American Psychological Association.

Campbell, D., & Fiske, D. (1959). Convergent and discriminant validation by the multitrait-multimethod matrix. *Psychological Bulletin, 56,* 81–105.

Committee on Ethical Guidelines for Forensic Psychologists (1991). Specialty guidelines for forensic psychologists. *Law and Human Behavior, 15,* 655–665.

Committee on Psychological Tests and Assessment (1996). *American Psychologist, 51,* 644–648.

Conroy, M. A. (2003). Evaluation of sexual predators. In A. M. Goldstein (Ed.), *Forensic psychology: Vol. 11* of *Handbook of psychology* (pp. 463–484). Hoboken, NJ: John Wiley & Sons.

Craig, R. K. (1999). When Daubert gets Erie: Medical certainty and medical expert testimony in federal court. *Denver University Law Review, 77,* 69–118.

Curran, W., McGarry, A., & Shah, S. (Eds.) (1986). *Forensic psychiatry and psychology.* Philadelphia, PA: F. A. Davis.

DeMatteo, D., & Edens, J. F. (2006). The role and relevance of the Psychopathy Checklist in court: A case law survey of U.S. courts (1991–2004). *Psychology, Public Policy and Law, 12,* 214–241.

Diamond, B. (1959). The fallacy of the impartial expert. *Archives of Criminal Psychodynamics, 3,* 221–230.

Drogin, Y. Y. (1999). Prophets in another land: Utilizing psychological expertise from foreign jurisdictions. *Mental and Physical Disabilities Law Reporter, 23,* 767–771.

Edens, J. F. (2001). Misuses of the Hare Psychopathy Checklist in court: Two case examples. *Journal of Interpersonal Violence, 16,* 1082–1093.

Ennis, B., & Litwack, T. (1974). Psychiatry and the presumption of expertise: Flipping coins in the courtroom. *California Law Review, 62,* 693–752.

Everington, C., & Luckasson, R. (1992). *Competence Assessment for Standing Trial for Defendants with Mental Retardation (CAST-MR): Test manual.* Worthington, OH: IDS Publishing Corporation.

Ewing, C. P. (2003). Expert testimony: Law and practice. In A. M. Goldstein (Ed.), *Forensic psychology: Vol. 11* of *Handbook of psychology* (pp. 55–68). Hoboken, NJ: John Wiley & Sons.

Faigman, D. L. (2006). The role of the judge in the twenty-first century: Judges as "amateur scientists." *Boston University Law Review, 86,* 1207–1225.

Gerbasi, J. (2004). Forensic assessment in personal injury litigation. In R. Simon & L. Gold (Eds.), *Textbook of forensic psychiatry* (pp. 231–261). Washington, D.C.: American Psychiatric Publishing.

Gold, L. (2004). Rediscovering forensic psychiatry. In R. Simon & L. Gold (Eds.), *Textbook of forensic psychiatry* (pp. 3–36). Washington, D.C.: American Psychiatric Publishing.

Golding, S., & Roesch, R., (1983). Interdisciplinary Fitness Interview training manual. Unpublished manuscript.

Golding, S., Roesch, R., & Schreiber, J. (1984). Assessment and conceptualization of competency to stand trial: Preliminary data on the Interdisciplinary Fitness Interview. *Law and Human Behavior, 9,* 321–334.

Goldstein, A. M. (Ed.) (2003a). *Forensic psychology: Vol. 11* of *Handbook of psychology.* Hoboken, NJ: John Wiley & Sons.

Goldstein, A. M. (2003b). Overview of forensic psychology. In A. M. Goldstein (Ed.), *Forensic psychology: Vol. 11* of *Handbook of psychology* (pp. 3–20). Hoboken, NJ: John Wiley & Sons.

Goldstein, A. M. (Ed.) (2007). *Forensic psychology: Emerging topics and expanding roles.* Hoboken, NJ: John Wiley and Sons.

Goldstein, A. M., Morse, S. J., & Shapiro, D. L. (2003). Evaluation of criminal responsibility. In A. M. Goldstein (Ed.), *Forensic psychology: Vol. 11* of *Handbook of psychology* (pp. 381–406). Hoboken, NJ: John Wiley & Sons.

Goldstein, J., Freud, A., & Solnit, A. (1973). *Beyond the best interests of the child.* New York: Free Press.

Greenberg, S. A. & Shuman, D. W. (1997). Irreconcilable conflict between therapeutic and forensic roles. *Professional Psychology: Research and Practice, 28,* 50–57.

Greenberg, S. A., Shuman, D. W., Feldman, S. R., Middleton, C., & Ewing, C. P. (2007). Lessons for forensic practice drawn from the law of malpractice. In A. M. Goldstein (Ed.), *Forensic psychology: Emerging topics and expanding roles* (pp. 446–464). Hoboken, NJ: John Wiley and Sons.

Greene, E., Heilbrun, K., Fortune, W., & Nietzel, M. (2006). *Wrightsman's psychology and the legal system* (6th edition). Belmont, CA:: Wadsworth.

Greene, R.L. (2007). Forensic applications of the Minnesota Multiphasic Personality Inventory-2. In A. M. Goldstein (Ed), *Forensic psychology: Emerging topics and expanding roles* (pp. 73–96). Hoboken, NJ: John Wiley and Sons.

Grisso, T. (1980). Juveniles' capacities to waive Miranda rights: An empirical analysis. *California Law Review, 68,* 1134–1166.

Grisso, T. (1981). *Juveniles' waiver of rights: Legal and psychological competence.* New York: Plenum.

Grisso, T. (1986a). *Evaluating competencies: Forensic assessments and instruments.* New York: Plenum.

Grisso, T. (1986b). Psychological assessment in legal contexts. In W. Curran, A. L. McGarry, & S. Shah (Eds.), *Forensic psychiatry and psychology: Perspectives and standards for interdisciplinary practice* (pp. 103–128). Philadelphia: Davis.

Grisso, T. (1988). *Competency to stand trial evaluations: A manual for practice.* Sarasota, FL: Professional Resource Press.

Grisso, T. (1991). A developmental history of the American Psychology-Law Society. *Law and Human Behavior, 15,* 213–231.

Grisso, T. (1997). Juvenile competency to stand trial: Questions in an era of punitive reform. *Criminal Justice, 12,* 4–11.

Grisso, T. (1998). *Forensic evaluation of juveniles*. Sarasota, FL: Professional Resource Press.

Grisso, T. (2003). *Evaluating competencies: Forensic assessments and instruments* (2nd edition). New York: Kluwer Academic/Plenum Press.

Grisso, T. (2005). *Double jeopardy: Adolescent offenders with mental disorders*. Chicago: University of Chicago Press.

Grisso, T. (2006). Foreword. In S. Sparta & G. Koocher (Eds.), *Forensic mental health assessment of children and adolescents*. New York: Oxford University Press.

Grisso, T., & Appelbaum, P. (1998a). *Assessing competence to consent to treatment: A guide for physicians and other health professionals*. New York: Oxford University Press.

Grisso, T., & Appelbaum, P. (1998b). *MacArthur Competence Assessment Tool for Treatment (MacCAT-T)*. Sarasota, FL: Professional Resource Press.

Grisso, T., & Steadman, H.J. (1995). Saleem A. Shah: The man and his imperative. *Law and Human Behavior, 19*, 1–3.

Grisso, T., Sales, B., & Bayless, S. (1982). Law-related graduate courses and programs in psychology departments: A national survey. *American Psychologist, 37*, 267–278.

Grisso, T., Vincent, G., & Seagrave, D. (2005). *Mental health screening and assessment in juvenile justice*. New York: Guilford.

Group for the Advancement of Psychiatry (1974). *Misuse of psychiatry in the criminal courts: Competency to stand trial*. New York: Committee on Psychiatry and Law.

Gutheil, T. (2004). The expert witness. In R. Simon & L. Gold (Eds.), *Textbook of forensic psychiatry* (pp. 75–89). Washington, D.C.: American Psychiatric Publishing.

Gutheil, T. (2005). The history of forensic psychiatry. *Journal of the American Academy of Psychiatry and Law, 33*, 259–262.

Gutheil, T., & Appelbaum, P. (1982). *Clinical handbook of psychiatry and the law*. New York: McGraw-Hill.

Gutheil, T., & Appelbaum, P. (2000). *Clinical handbook of psychiatry and the law* (3rd edition). Baltimore: Lippincott, Williams & Wilkins.

Hare, R. (1991). *The Revised Psychopathy Checklist*. Toronto, CA: Multi-Health Systems.

Harris, G., & Rice, M. (2003). Actuarial assessment of risk among sex offenders. *Annals of the New York Academy of Sciences, 989*, 198–210.

Healy, W. (1923). *The individual delinquent*. Boston: Little, Brown.

Heilbrun, K. (1992). The role of psychological testing in forensic assessment. *Law and Human Behavior, 16*, 257–272.

Heilbrun, K. (March, 1996). *Daubert and forensic mental health assessment: Use and implications*. Presented at the Biennial Conference of the American Psychology-Law Society, Hilton Head, SC.

Heilbrun, K. (2001). *Principles of forensic mental health assessment*. New York: Kluwer Academic/Plenum Publishers.

Heilbrun, K. (2003). Principles of forensic mental health assessment: Implications for the forensic assessment of sexual offenders. In R.A. Prentky,

E. Janus, & M.E. Seto (Eds.), *Sexually coercive behavior: Understanding and management* (pp. 1–18). New York: Annals of the New York Academy of Sciences, Volume 989.

Heilbrun, K., & Collins, S. (1995). Evaluations of trial competency and mental state at the time of the offense: Report characteristics. *Professional Psychology: Research and Practice, 26,* 61–67.

Heilbrun, K., DeMatteo, D., & Marczyk, G. (2004). Pragmatic psychology, forensic mental health assessment, and the case of Thomas Jefferson: Applying principles to promote quality. *Psychology, Public Policy, and Law, 10,* 31–70.

Heilbrun, K., DeMatteo, D., Marczyk, G., & Goldstein, A. M. (in press). Toward informing a standard of care in forensic mental health assessment: Legal, professional, and principles-based consideration. *Psychology, Public Policy, and Law.*

Heilbrun, K., DeMatteo, D., Marczyk, G., Finello, C., Smith, R., & Mack-Allen, J. (2005). Applying principles of forensic mental health assessment to capital sentencing. *Widener Law Review, 11,* 93–118.

Heilbrun, K., Marczyk, G., & DeMatteo, D. (2002). *Forensic mental health assessment: A casebook.* New York: Oxford University Press.

Heilbrun, K., Marczyk, G., DeMatteo, D., & Mack-Allen, J. (2007). A principles-based approach to forensic mental health assessment: Utility and update. In A. M. Goldstein (ed), *Forensic psychology: Emerging topics and expanding roles* (pp. 45–72). Hoboken, NJ: John Wiley and Sons.

Heilbrun, K., Marczyk, G., DeMatteo, D., Zillmer, E., Harris, J., & Jennings, T. (2003). Principles of forensic mental health assessment: Implications for neuropsychological assessment in forensic contexts. *Assessment, 10,* 329–343.

Heilbrun, K., Rogers, R., & Otto, R. (2002). Forensic assessment: Current status and future directions. In J. Ogloff (Ed.), *Psychology and law: Reviewing the discipline* (pp. 120–147). New York: Kluwer Academic/Plenum Press.

Heilbrun, K., Warren, J., & Picarello, K. (2003). Third party information in forensic assessment. In Goldstein, A. M. (Ed.), *Forensic psychology: Vol. 11* of *Handbook of psychology,* (pp. 69–86). Hoboken, NJ: John Wiley & Sons.

Hess, A., & Weiner, I. (Eds.) (1999). *Handbook of forensic psychology* (2nd edition). New York: John Wiley & Sons.

Hoge, R., & Andrews, D. (2002). *Youth level of service/case management inventory: User's manual.* North Tonawanda, NY: Multi-Health Systems.

Horvath, L., Logan, T., & Walker, R. (2002). Child custody cases: A content analysis of evaluations in practice. *Professional Psychology: Research and Practice, 33,* 557–565.

Jesness, C., & Wedge, R. (1984). Validity of a revised Jesness Inventory I-Level classification with delinquents. *Journal of Consulting and Clinical Psychology, 52,* 997–1010.

Jones, K. (1999). *Taming the troublesome child: American families, child guidance, and the limits of psychiatric authority.* Cambridge, MA: Harvard University Press.

Kraemer, H., Kazdin, A., Offord, D., Kessler, R., Jensen, P., & Kupfer, D. (1997). Coming to terms with the terms of risk. *Archives of General Psychiatry, 54,* 337–343.

Laboratory of Community Psychiatry, Harvard Medical School (1973). *Competency to stand trial and mental illness* (DHEW Publication No. ADM77–103). Rockville, MD:

Lally, S. (2003). What tests are acceptable for use in forensic evaluations? A survey of experts. *Professional Psychology: Research and Practice, 34,* 491–498.

Lander, T. (2006). The content and quality of forensic mental health assessment: Validation of a principles-based approach. Unpublished doctoral dissertation, Drexel University, Philadelphia, PA.

Lewin, J. (1998). The genesis and evolution of legal uncertainty about reasonable medical certainty. *Maryland Law Review, 57,* 380–504.

Lidz, C., Mulvey, E., & Gardner, W. (1993). The accuracy of predictions of violence to others. *Journal of the American Medical Association, 269,* 1007–1011.

Marczyk, G., DeMatteo, D., Kutinsky, J., & Heilbrun, K. (2007). Training in forensic assessment and intervention. In R. L. Jackson (Ed.), *Learning forensic psychology* (pp. 3–32). New York: Routledge.

Marczyk, G., Knauss, L., Kutinsky, J., DeMatteo, D., & Heilbrun, K. (2007). The legal, ethical, and applied aspects of capital mitigation evaluations: Practice guidance from a principles-based approach. In H. Hall (Ed.), *Forensic psychology and neuropsychology for criminal and civil cases* (pp. 41–92, 779–792). New York: Taylor & Francis, CRC Press.

Marson, D., Cody, H., Ingram, K., & Harrell, L. (1995). Neuropsychological predictors of competency in Alzheimer's disease using a rational reasons legal standard. *Archives of Neurology, 52,* 955–959.

McGarry, A., Curran, W., & Kenefick, D. (1968). Problems of public consultation in medico-legal matters: A symposium. *American Journal of Psychiatry, 125,* 42–45.

Melton, G., Petrila, J., Poythress, N., & Slobogin, C. (1987). *Psychological evaluations for the courts: A handbook for mental health professionals and lawyers.* New York: Guilford.

Melton, G., Petrila, J., Poythress, N., & Slobogin, C. (1997). *Psychological evaluations for the courts: A handbook for mental health professionals and lawyers* (2nd edition). New York: Guilford.

Melton, G., Petrila, J., Poythress, N., & Slobogin, C. (2007). *Psychological evaluations for the courts: A handbook for mental health professionals and lawyers* (3rd edition). New York: Guilford.

Mental Retardation and Developmental Disabilities (no date). Guidelines on effective behavioral treatment for persons with mental retardation and developmental disabilities. http://www.apa.org.divisions/div33/effectivetreatment.html.

Messer, S. B. (2004). Evidence-based practice: Beyond empirically supported treatments. *Professional Psychology: Research and Practice, 35,* 580–588.

Monahan, J. (Ed.) (1980). *Who is the client? The ethics of psychological intervention in the criminal justice system.* Washington, D.C.: American Psychological Association.

Monahan, J. (1981). *The clinical prediction of violent behavior.* Washington, D.C.: Government Printing Office (DHHS Publication Number ADM 81–921).

Monahan, J. (2003). Violence risk assessment. In A. M. Goldstein (Ed.), *Forensic psychology: Vol. 11* of *Handbook of psychology,* (pp. 527–542). Hoboken, NJ: John Wiley & Sons.

Monahan, J., & Walker, L. (1985). *Social science in law.* Westbury, NY: The Foundation Press.

Monahan, J., & Walker, L. (2006). *Social science in law* (6th edition). Westbury, NY: The Foundation Press.

Monahan, J., Steadman, H., Silver, E., Appelbaum, A., Robbins, P., Mulvey, E., et al. (2001). *Rethinking risk assessment: The MacArthur study of mental disorder and violence.* New York: Oxford University Press.

Monahan, J., Steadman, J., Appelbaum, P., Grisso, T., Mulvey, E., Roth, L., et al. (2005). *Classification of Violence Risk (COVR).* Lutz, FL: Psychological Assessment Resources.

Morey, L. C., Warner, M. B., & Hopwood, C. J. (2007). The Personality Assessment Inventory: Issues in legal and forensic settings. In A. M. Goldstein (Ed.), *Forensic psychology: Emerging topics and expanding roles* (pp. 97–126). Hoboken, NJ: John Wiley and Sons.

Morse, S. (1978). Law and mental health professionals: The limits of expertise. *Professional Psychology, 9,* 389–399.

Morse, S. (1982). Reforming expert testimony: An open response from the tower (and the trenches). *Law and Human Behavior, 6,* 45–47.

Morse, S. (1999). Crazy reasons. *Journal of Contemporary Legal Issues, 10,* 189–226.

Mossman, D. (2004). Understanding prediction instruments. In R. Simon & L. Gold (Eds.), *Textbook of forensic psychiatry* (pp. 501–523). Washington, D.C.: American Psychiatric Publishing.

Mossman, D., Noffsinger, S., Ash, P., Frierson, R., Gerbasi, J., Hackett, M., et al. (2007). AAPL practice guideline for the forensic psychiatric evaluation of competence to stand trial. *Journal of the American Academy of Psychiatry and the Law, 35,* S3–S72.

Nicholson, R., & Norwood, S. (2000). The quality of forensic psychological assessments, reports, and testimony: Acknowledging the gap between promise and practice. *Law and Human Behavior, 24,* 9–44.

Nicholson, R., Robertson, H., Johnson, W., & Jensen, G. (1988). A comparison of instruments for assessing competence to stand trial. *Law and Human Behavior, 12,* 313–321.

Norcross, J. C., Beutler, L. E., & Levant, R. F. (Eds.) (2006). *Evidenced-based practice in mental health: Debate and dialogue on fundamental questions.* Washington, D.C.: American Psychological Association.

O'Donahue, W., & Bradley, A. (1999). Conceptual and empirical issues in child custody evaluations. *Clinical Psychology: Science and Practice, 6,* 310–322.

Otto, R., & Edens, J. (2003). Parenting capacity. In T. Grisso (Ed.), *Evaluating competencies: Forensic assessments and instruments* (2nd edition). New York: Kluwer Academic/Plenum Publishers.

Otto, R. K., & Heilbrun, K. (2002). The practice of forensic psychology: A look toward the future in light of the past. *American Psychologist, 57,* 5–18.

Otto, R., Heilbrun, K., & Grisso, T. (1990). Training and credentialing in forensic psychology. *Behavioral Sciences and the Law, 8,* 217–231.

Otto, R. K., Slobogin, C., & Greenberg, S. A. (2007). Legal and ethical issues in accessing and utilizing third-party information. In A. M. Goldstein (Ed.), *Forensic psychology: Emerging topics and expanding roles* (pp. 190–208). Hoboken, NJ: John Wiley and Sons.

Packer, I. K., & Borum, R. (2003). Forensic training and practice. In A. M. Goldstein, (Ed.), *Forensic psychology: Vol. 11* of *Handbook of psychology,* (pp. 21–32). Hoboken, NJ: John Wiley & Sons.

Pope, K. S., & Vetter, V. A. (1992). Ethical dilemmas encountered by members of the American Psychological Association. *American Psychologist, 47,* 397–411.

Poythress, N. L. (1982). Concerning reform in expert testimony: An open letter from a practicing psychologist. *Law and Human Behavior, 6,* 39–43.

Poythress, N., Nicholson, R., Otto, R., Edens, J., Bonnie, R., Monahan, J., & Hoge, S. (1999). *The MacArthur Competence Assessment Tool—Criminal Adjudication: Professional manual.* Odessa, FL: Psychological Assessment Resources.

Quay, H. (1966). Personality patterns in preadolescent delinquent boys. *Educational and Psychological Measurement, 16,* 99–110.

Quay, H., (1987). Patterns of delinquent behavior. In H. Quay (Ed.), *Handbook of juvenile delinquency* (pp. 118–138). New York: John Wiley.

Quinsey, V., Harris, G., Rice, M., & Cormier, C. (1998). *Violent offenders: Appraising and managing risk.* Washington, D.C.: American Psychological Association.

Quinsey, V., Harris, G., Rice, M., & Cormier, C. (2006). *Violent offenders: Appraising and managing risk* (2nd edition). Washington, D.C.: American Psychological Association.

Reed, G. M., Kihlstrom, J. F., & Messer, S. B. (2006). What qualifies as evidence of effective practice? In J. C. Norcross, L. E. Beutler, & R. F. Levant (Eds.), *Evidence-based practice in mental health: Debate and dialogue on fundamental questions* (pp. 13–55). Washington, D.C.: American Psychological Association.

Ribner, H. (2002). *The handbook of juvenile forensic psychology.* Hoboken, NJ: Jossey-Bass.

Roesch, R., & Golding, S. (1980). *Competency to stand trial.* Champaign-Urbana, IL: University of Illinois Press.

Roesch, R., Zapf, P., Eaves, D., & Webster, C. (1998). *Fitness Interview Test (Revised Edition).* Burnaby, British Columbia, Canada: Mental Health, Law and Policy Institute, Simon Fraser University.

Rogers, R. (1984). *Rogers Criminal Responsibility Assessment Scales.* Odessa, FL: Psychological Assessment Resources.

Rogers, R. (1986). *Conducting insanity evaluations.* New York: Van Nostrand Reinhold.

Rogers, R. (Ed.) (1988). *Clinical assessment of malingering and deception.* New York: Guilford.

Rogers, R. (Ed.) (1997). *Clinical assessment of malingering and deception* (2nd edition). New York: Guilford Press.

Rogers, R., & Bender, S. D. (2003). Evaluation of malingering and deception. In A. M. Goldstein (Ed.), *Forensic psychology: Vol. 11* of *Handbook of psychology* (pp. 109–132). Hoboken, NJ: John Wiley & Sons.

Rogers, R., & Ewing, C. P. (1989). Ultimate opinion proscriptions: A cosmetic fix and a plea for empiricism. *Law and Human Behavior, 13,* 357–374.

Rogers, R., & Shuman, D. (2000). *Conducting insanity evaluations* (2nd edition). New York: Guilford.

Rogers, R., Tillbrook, C., & Sewell, K. (2003). *Evaluation of Competence to Stand Trial-Revised.* Lutz, FL: Psychological Assessment Resources.

Rosner, R. (1983). Education and training in forensic psychiatry. *Psychiatric Clinics of North America, 6,* 585.

Rosner, R. (2003) (Ed.). *Principles and practice of forensic psychiatry* (2nd edition). New York: Oxford University Press.

Rosner, R., & Harmon, R. (1989). *Criminal court consultation.* New York: Plenum.

Roth, L., Meisel, A., & Lidz, C. (1977). Tests of competency to consent to treatment. *American Journal of Psychiatry, 134,* 279–284.

Roth, L., Lidz, C, Meisel, A., Soloff, P., Kaufman, F., Spiker, D.,et al. (1982). Competency to decide about treatment or research: An overview of some empirical data. *International Journal of Law and Psychiatry, 5,* 29–50.

Ryba, N. L., Cooper, V. G., & Zapf, P. A. (2003). Juvenile competence to stand trial evaluations: A survey of current practices and test usage among psychologists. *Professional Psychology: Research and Practice, 34,* 499–507.

Saks, M., & Baron, C. (1980). *The use/nonuse/misuse of applied social research in the courts.* Cambridge, MA: Abt Books.

Salekin, R. (2004). *Risk-Sophistication-Treatment Inventory: Professional manual.* Lutz, FL: Psychological Assessment Resources.

Schetky, D., & Benedek, E. (Eds.) (1980). *Child psychiatry and the law.* New York: Brunner/Mazel.

Schetky, D., & Benedek, E. (2002). *Principles and practice of child and adolescent forensic psychiatry.* Washington, D.C.: American Psychiatry Press.

Schutz, B., Dixon, E., Lindenberger, J., & Ruther, N. (1989). *Solomon's sword: A practical guide to conducting child custody evaluations.* San Francisco, CA: Jossey-Bass.

Shapiro, D. (1984). *Psychological evaluations and expert testimony: A practical guide for forensic work.* New York: Van Nostrand-Reinhold.

Shapiro, D. (1991). *Forensic psychological assessment: An integrative approach.* Boston: Allyn & Bacon.

Shuman, D. (1986). *Psychiatric and psychological evidence.* New York: McGraw-Hill.

Shuman, D. (2004). Introduction to the legal system. In R. Simon & L. Gold (Eds.), *Textbook of forensic psychiatry* (pp. 37–54). Washington, D.C.: American Psychiatric Publishing.

Shuman, D. (2005). *Psychiatric and psychological evidence.* St. Paul, MN: Thomson-West.

Shuman, D., Cunningham, M., Connell, M., & Reid, W. (2003). Interstate forensic psychological consultations: A call for reform and proposal of a model rule. *Professional Psychology: Research and Practice, 34,* 233–239.

Simon, R., & Gold, L. (Eds.) (2004a). *Textbook of forensic psychiatry.* Washington, D.C.: American Psychiatric Publishing.

Simon, R., & Gold, L. (2004b). Psychiatric diagnosis in litigation. In R. Simon & L. Gold (Eds.), *Textbook of forensic psychiatry.* Washington, D.C.: American Psychiatric Publishing.

Skeem, J., & Golding, S. (1998). Community examiner's evaluations of competence to stand trial: Common problems and suggestions for improvement. *Professional Psychology: Research and Practice, 29,* 357–367.

Skeem, J., Golding, S., Cohn, N., & Berge, G. (1998). Logic and reliability of evaluations of competence to stand trial. *Law and Human Behavior, 22,* 519–547.

Slobogin, C. (1989). The ultimate issue issue. *Behavioral Sciences and the Law, 7,* 259–268.

Society for Industrial and Organizational Psychology. (2003). *Validation and use of personnel selection procedures* (4th edition). Bowling Green, OH: Society for Industrial and Organizational Psychology.

Stone, A. (1975). *Mental health and law: A system in transition* (DHEW Public, No. ADM-75-176). Rockville, MD: National Institute of Mental Health.

Tepper, A., & Elwork, A. (1984). Competence to consent to treatment as a psycholegal construct. *Law and Human Behavior, 8,* 205–223.

Thompson, J., LeBourgeois, H., & Black, F. (2004). Malingering. In R. Simon & L. Gold (Eds.), *Textbook of forensic psychiatry* (pp. 427–448). Washington, D.C.: American Psychiatric Publishing.

Tillbrook, C., Mumley, D., & Grisso, T. (2003). Avoiding expert opinions on the ultimate legal question: The case for integrity. *Journal of Forensic Psychology Practice, 3,* 77–87.

Tippins, T., & Wittman, J. (2005). Empirical and ethical problems with child custody recommendations: A call for clinical humility and judicial vigilance. *Family Court Review, 43,* 193–222.

Tucillo, J., DeFilippis, N., Denny, R., & Dsurney, J. (2002). Licensure requirements for interjurisdictional forensic evaluations. *Professional Psychology: Research and Practice, 33,* 377–383.

Van Gorp, W. (2007). Neuropsychology for the forensic psychologist. In A. M. Goldstein (Ed.), *Forensic psychology: Emerging topics and expanding roles* (pp. 154–170). Hoboken, NJ: John Wiley and Sons.

Warren, M. (1976). Intervention with juvenile delinquents. In M. Rosenheim (Ed.), *Pursuing justice for the child* (pp. 176–204). Chicago: University of Chicago Press.

Weiner, I. (2007). Rorschach assessment in forensic cases. In A. M. Goldstein (Ed.), *Forensic psychology: Emerging topics and expanding roles*, (pp. 127–153). Hoboken, NJ: John Wiley and Sons.

Weiner, I., & Hess, A. (Eds.) (1987). *The handbook of forensic psychology*. New York: John Wiley.

Weiner, I., & Hess, A. (Eds.) (2005). *The handbook of forensic psychology* (3rd edition). New York: John Wiley.

Weinstock, R., & Gold, L. (2004). Ethics in forensic psychiatry. In R. Simon & L. Gold (Eds.), *Textbook of forensic psychiatry* (pp. 91–115). Washington, D.C.: American Psychiatric Publishing.

Weissman, H., & DeBow, D. (2003). Ethical principles and professional competencies. In A. M. Goldstein (Ed.), *Forensic psychology: Vol. 11* of *Handbook of psychology*, (pp. 33–54). Hoboken, NJ: John Wiley & Sons.

Weithorn, L., & Campbell, S. (1982). The competency of children and adolescents to make informed treatment decisions. *Child Development, 53,* 1589–1599.

Wettstein, R. (2004). The forensic examination and report. In R. Simon & L. Gold (Eds.), *Textbook of forensic psychiatry* (pp. 139–164). Washington, D.C.: American Psychiatric Publishing.

Wettstein, R. (2005). Quality and quality improvement in forensic mental health evaluations. *Journal of the American Academy of Psychiatry and the Law, 33,* 158–175.

Wildman, R., Batchelor, E., Thompson, L., Nelson, F., Moore, J., Patterson, M.,et al. (1980). The Georgia Court Competence Test: An attempt to develop a rapid, quantitative measure for fitness for trial. Unpublished manuscript, Forensic Services Division, Central State Hospital, Milledgeville, GA.

Wrightsman, L. (1987). *Psychology and the legal system*. Pacific Grove, CA: Brooks/Cole.

Wrightsman, L., Nietzel, M., Fortune, W., & Greene, E. (2001). *Psychology and the legal system* (3rd edition). Pacific Grove, CA: Brooks/Cole.

Yantz, C., Bauer, L., & McCaffrey, R. (2006). Regulations governing out-of-state practice of psychology: Implications for forensic neuropsychologists. *Applied Neuropsychology, 13,* 19–27.

Ziskin, J. (1970). *Coping with psychiatric and psychological testimony*. Beverly Hills, CA: Law and Psychology Press.

Ziskin, J., & Faust, D. (1995). *Coping with psychiatric and psychological testimony* (5th edition). Beverly Hills, CA: Law and Psychology Press.

Zonana, H., Roth, J.A., & Coric, V. (2004). Forensic assessment of sex offenders. In R. Simon & L. Gold (Eds.), *Textbook of forensic psychiatry* (pp. 349–375). Washington, D.C.: American Psychiatric Publishing.

Cases and Statutes

Atkins v. Virginia, 536 U.S. 304 (2002).

Barefoot v. Estelle, 463 U.S. 880 (1983).

Crawford v. Washington, 541 U.S. 36 (2004).

Dusky v. United States, 362 U.S. 402 (1960).

Daubert v. Merrell Dow Pharmaceuticals, 509 U.S. 579 (1993).

Federal Rule of Evidence 702–704.

Frye v. United States, 293 F. 1013 (D.C. Cir. 1923).

General Electric Company et al. v. Joiner et ux., 522 U.S. 136 (1997).

Hahn v. Union Pacific Railroad, IL Appellate Court, 5th District, No. 5–03–0466, decision filed 09–24–04.

In re Gault, 387 U.S. 1 (1967).

Insanity Defense Reform Act (1984). Pub. L. 98–473, 18 U.S.C. 401–406.

Jenkins v. United States, 307 F.2d 637 (U.S. App. D.C., 1962).

People v. Goldstein, 2005 WL 3477726 (NY).

Rogers v. Okin, 478 F. Supp. 1342 (1979).

Roper v. Simmons, 543 U.S. 551 (2005).

United States v. Bramlet, 820 F.2d 851 (7th Cir. 1987).

United States v. Cameron, 9075 F.2d 1051 (11th Cir. 1990).

United States v. Childress, 585 F.3d. 693 (D.C. Cir. 1995).

United States v. Pohlot, 827 F.2d 889 (3rd Cir. 1987).

United States v. Sims, 514 F.2d 147 (9th Cir. 1973).

United States v. Wright, 783 F. 2d (D.C. Cir. 1986).

Zinermon v. Burch, 494 U.S. 113 (1990).

Index

About the Authors

Kirk Heilbrun, PhD, is currently Professor and Head of the Department of Psychology, Drexel University. His current research focuses on juvenile and adult offenders, legal decision-making, and forensic evaluation associated with such decision-making. He is the author of a number of articles on forensic assessment, violence risk assessment and risk communication, and the treatment of mentally disordered offenders, and has published four books (*Principles of Forensic Mental Health Assessment*, 2001; *Forensic Mental Health Assessment: A Casebook*, with Geff Marczyk and Dave DeMatteo, 2002; *Juvenile Delinquency: Prevention, Assessment, and Intervention*, with Naomi Goldstein and Rich Redding, 2005; and *Wrightsman's Psychology and the Legal System*, 6th edition, with Edie Greene, Mike Nietzel, and Bill Fortune, 2006). His practice interests also center around forensic assessment, and he directs a clinic within the department in this area. He is board certified in Clinical Psychology and in Forensic Psychology by the American Board of Professional Psychology, and has previously served as president of both the American Psychology-Law Psychology/APA Division 41, and the American Board of Forensic Psychology. He received the 2004 Distinguished Contributions to Forensic Psychology award from the American Academy of Forensic Psychology.

Thomas Grisso, PhD, is Professor, Director of Psychology, and Director of the Law and Psychiatry Program at the University of Massachusetts Medical School. His research has examined the application of psychological assessment to questions of legal competencies, and application of clinical and developmental psychology to law, policy, and practice in juvenile justice. Among his ten books are *Evaluating Competencies* (1986, 2003), *Forensic Evaluation of Juveniles* (1998), *Youth on Trial* (2000, edited with R. Schwartz), and *Double Jeopardy: Adolescent Offenders with Mental Disorders* (2004). He has received the American Psychological Association's award for Distinguished Contributions to Research in Public Policy (1994), an honorary Doctor of Laws degree from the John Jay College of

Criminal Justice, City University of New York (1998), the American Psychiatric Association's Isaac Ray Award (2005), and the U.K.'s Royal College of Psychiatrists Honorary Fellow Award (2006). He has received the American Board of Professional Psychology's Award for Distinguished Contributions (2002) and currently is Executive Director of the American Board of Forensic Psychology.

Alan M. Goldstein, PhD, is Professor of Psychology on the graduate faculty of John Jay College of Criminal Justice and on the doctoral faculty of the Clinical Psychology Ph.D. Program of the Graduate Center—City University of New York. He chaired the Continuing Education Program of the American Academy of Forensic Psychology for 18 years and again serves as co-chair of that program. He is a Director of the American Board of Forensic Psychology, served as Chair of the Ethics Committee of the American Board of Professional Psychology, and was Chair of APA's Continuing Professional Education Committee. Dr. Goldstein was a member of the Board of Trustees of the American Board of Professional Psychology. He is editor of *Forensic Psychology* (2003) and *Forensic Psychology: Emerging Topics and Expanding Roles* (2007). Dr. Goldstein is the recipient of the American Academy of Forensic Psychology's 1997 Distinguished Contribution Award to the Field of Forensic Psychology. He was named the "2000 Continuing Education Distinguished Speaker" by the American Psychological Association. He received the Beth Clark Distinguished Service Award to Forensic Psychology in 2006, awarded by the American Board of Forensic Psychology and in 2007, he received the Distinguished Contribution Award to the American Board of Professional Psychology.